SINGING
BLACKBIRDS

Also available from Grey House in the Woods

the Voice within the Wind
of Becoming and the Druid Way
Greywind

the Path through the Forest
a Druid Guidebook
Julie White & Graeme K Talboys

Arianrhod's Dance
a Druid Ritual Handbook
Julie White & Graeme K Talboys

Wealden Hill
a novel
Graeme K Talboys

SINGING WITH BLACKBIRDS

The Survival of Primal Celtic
Shamanism in later Folk-Traditions

Stuart A. Harris-Logan

Grey House in the Woods

First published on the Summer Solstice 2006 by
Grey House in the Woods
PO Box 8211
Girvan
Ayrshire
KA26 0WA
Scotland
www.greyhouseinthewoods.org

ISBN 0-9540531-6-8

Set in 11 point Times New Roman by Greywind
Cover by Greywind

Acknowledgements

To the spirits, for their support, guidance and inspiration.

To my family, both here and yonder, for their encouragement.

To Dr Geo Trevarthen, for laying a path through the forest.

To Graeme Talboys for many useful and practical suggestions.

To Glasgow University Library for buying the books I needed.

And to the blackbirds, whose song created my branch of the tradition.

o0o

To all my friends and colleagues who have helped in numerous ways, particularly to Rob Westwood, Frank MacEowen, Claire Hewitt, *Fionn Tulach*, Richard Bapty, David Clement, Fiona Neale, Diane Carnochan, Anne Wright, and Louise Annan: you have all helped immensely, even if you weren't aware of it at the time. There are also so many more people to thank, you know who you are – apologies for leaving you out.

Agus thusa fhithich, mo riochd, le graidh agus beannachdan.

Tapadh leibh uile.

The author and the publisher would like to thank the owners of www.firstpeople.us and www.buryatmongol.com for their kind permission to reproduce photographs from their sites.

CONTENTS

Introduction
    'And so let the druids sing . . .'   ix

Part One – *Druids and Drums: The Instruments of Ecstasy*
    Laying the Foundation Stone   3
    Am torc ar gáill...   9
    In Flight to the Spirits   14
    Reinventing the Wheel   27
    Stone on top of stone, and the wall goes up...   35

Part Two – *Gaining Possession of a Sacrality*
    Be you a smooth way before me...   43
    Into the Mist   45
    Exstasis in Sacred Practice   55
    Uses of Shamanic Consciousness   62
    A Culturally Supported Schizophrenia?   67
    Finding a Language   72

Part Three – *A Shaman in the Gàidhealtachd?*
    The Voice of the Elements   79
    Riochd nan Daoine   82
    The Language of Birds   87
    ri traghadh 's ri lionadh   94
    Gaelic Chant and Possession   101
    Túathcháech and the Gaelic Sucking Doctor   109
    Binding the Threads   117

Conclusion
    'To the end of ends...'   121

Dancing with Ravens
    A Case Study of Gaelic Shamanism   125

Apologia
    'On Bananas and the Nature of Celtic Shamanism'   133

Notes   139

Select Bibliography   151

Index   163

INTRODUCTION

'And so let the druids sing . . .'

> life stirs
> light stirs us all
> and an eagle soars toward the sun
> on the sighs of our awakening…
> – Josie Tamarin 'song for the journey'

[handwritten annotation: 1 Shamanka = female shaman *]*

T he shaman[1] is a specialist in the Sacred, a practitioner of ancient techniques of ecstasy. To the shaman, the spirits are a vital and sustaining presence whose help can be sought in times of spiritual or material crisis. As representatives of and for their communities, shamans must maintain the balance between the two worlds; the corporeal and the spiritual.

In Old Irish literature (as in Scottish and Welsh traditions), interaction with the *Aes Side*, or spirit people, is depicted as commonplace. In later times, when overtly pagan Celtic customs became increasingly persecuted, such practices became, in many cases, less codified and more personal. Despite this, we continue to see an interaction with the spirits in the folklore, mythology and hagiography incorporated into later spiritual movements.

Bringing together the fields of anthropology and Celtic studies feels rather like reuniting two long-lost relatives; perhaps one reason why this field of research has not been given the credence and resources it deserves. Positing the thesis that the Celts may have employed shamanistic visionary practices and techniques is not new, however. Pokorny first made the comparison in 1908, and Piggot again in 1962.[2]

It is the focus of this study to investigate such comparisons with an academic eye, in order to ascertain whether or not they stand up to scrutiny. In order to do so, however, it is first necessary to define exactly what is meant by the terms 'Celtic' and 'shamanic'.

o0o

Who were the Celts? As a people, the Celts have proven to be very difficult to pin down and identify. Champion argues that 'it is not currently possible to prove that any of the Iron Age peoples who lived in central or western Europe definitely spoke a Celtic language or defined themselves as Celts.'[3] While this may be so, it is also likely that a close kinship would have existed between tribes which are now considered to be Celtic, even if they did not adopt the same ethnonyms that the classical authors used for them.

Textually, the earliest references to the tribes the Greeks called *Keltoi* places them in central Europe, south-western Iberia and around the Danube's source from the 6th to the 4th centuries BCE. Materially, the first cultures that archaeologists have come to identify as Celtic are the Halstatt (7th – 5th centuries BCE) and La Tène (5th – 1st centuries BCE) 'type-sites'. Considering such vast amounts of geography over such an extended period of time puts paid to any notion of a single, unified and definitive Celtic culture.

Despite this elusiveness, however, there are enduring linguistic connections between groups which have been considered Celtic. Cunliffe speculates that the Celtic language group diverged from Italic some time between 1300 and 800 BCE, before the outward migration of the two peoples.[4] *P-Celtic* (the father of Welsh, Cornish and Breton) and *Q-Celtic* (the father of Irish, Manx and Scots Gaelic) both find their roots around this time. Where language commonalities exist, it is reasonable to assume that cultural and spiritual commonalities exist also.

The classical authors appear to use the term 'Celtic' in both the ethnic and linguistic senses, however they never appear to apply it to the British Isles. Celtic language inscriptions, place-names, ethnonyms and personal names in Switzerland, Italy, France and Spain gives a strong indication of Celtic migration into these areas from 600 BCE onwards,[5] and points towards a Celtic presence in Britain and Ireland.

We can see evidence for this in a number of places. Firstly, tribal names such as the *Atrebates* and the *Parisii* are identified on both sides of the English Channel. Secondly, classical authors report similarities between continental and insular tribes in Europe:

> ... observers like Caesar and Tacitus refer to linguistic, cultural and political links between Britain and the Continent, including the Druids of Gaul going to Britain for further study, and to similarities 'in the character and customs of the people' (ingenia cultusque hominum) between Britain and Ireland. These are telling facts for an 'objectivist' ethnologist, and undermine ... [a] ... 'subjectivist' deduction that 'there is no logic in calling the indigenous inhabitants of the British Isles 'Celts'.[6]

Finally, we know from more recent history that the descendants of P and Q Celtic languages found their way to the British Isles. Without some migration into these areas, it would be difficult to see how this would have happened. With the spread of language, it is reasonable also to assume a concomitant spread of cultural and spiritual values. Sims-Williams supports this view, reporting that 'Celtic language and Celtic ethnicity ... often go together.'[7]

In the end we are left with a rather vague classification; that the Celts were a grouping of tribes living in Asia Minor, Europe and the British Isles (including Ireland), speaking related languages of Proto-Celtic derivation, and sharing a number of cultural commonalities. In addition to this, we may also assume that a certain homogeneity in religious and spiritual practice would have been in evidence. In referring to the terms 'Celt' or 'Celtic' in this study, I refer to these commonalities.

o0o

The term 'shaman' comes to us from the Tungusic language of Siberia. *Šaman,* thought to denote one who is 'excited, moved, raised', is also related to a word meaning 'to know'[8] In recent times, anthropologists have adopted the term to refer to individuals who perform a vast number of practices across a wide range of cultures. Eliade, attempting to pin this down, arrives at one simple conclusion: 'shamanism = *technique of ecstasy*'.[9]

Exstasis, literally 'out-of-state' or alternative state of consciousness, fosters a feeling of uninhibited bliss in the shaman; a technique which allows him to enter into trance and journey into non-material existences. One Iglulik Eskimo shaman's account of reaching *exstasis* describes the feeling as akin to an 'inexplicable joy, a joy so powerful that I could not restrain it, but had to break into song, a mighty song, with only room for the one word: joy, joy!'[10]

Eliade warns, however, that shamanism must be 'taken in its strict and exact sense ... [as] ... pre-eminently a religious phenomenon'. Not any ecstatic can be classified as a shaman, as the latter 'specializes in a trance during which his soul is believed to leave his body and ascend to the sky or descend to the underworld.'[11] We arrive at the definition, then, that a shaman is a specialist in trance who utilises ecstatic techniques to interact with spirits and deities on behalf of his community.

Anthropologists are in general agreement that shamanistic cultures usually adopt an animistic world-view. Such a philosophy supposes a spiritual awareness to natural objects and occurrences, attributing 'life or divinity to such natural phenomena as trees, thunder, or celestial bodies.'[12] This perspective is consistent with the accepted view of primal Celtic spirituality also:

> It is generally accepted that the basic perception underpinning the religion of the pagan Celts was that the gods were everywhere: the landscape was full of spirits. Thus, every tree, spring, lake, river and mountain was numinous. All over Celtic Europe, there is evidence of

the very close association between the Celts and their natural world which was, to them, full of supernatural energy, energy which could do humankind good or evil, and therefore needed to be controlled or neutralised.[13]

In classically shamanic cultures, it is the role of the shaman to 'control' or 'neutralise' such unseen spiritual forces. In ancient Celtic times, this function would have been the preserve of the druids.

In describing the ecstatic phenomenon, Eliade listed what he considered to be the key characteristics pertaining to the shaman's profession: '…he is believed to cure, like all doctors, and to perform miracles of the fakir type, like all magicians, whether primitive or modern. But beyond this, he is a psychopomp, and he may also be a priest, mystic and poet.'[14] This compares strikingly to a description of the druids given by Julius Caesar, who identifies their role as priest, law-giver, psychopomp[15] and poet. Pliny the Elder fleshes out this description, indicating that they also perform the functions of diviner and physician.

In his comprehensive study of the subject, Mircea Eliade details a number of features which can be used to identify a typical shaman. Generally, the shaman is 'called' to their vocation by the spirits. Often this can be a traumatic as well as transformative experience, and often involves some kind of symbolic ritual death. After experiencing the otherworld through this psycho-spiritual ordeal, the shaman learns how to build upon his initial contact by travelling into the spirit world at will. This is often achieved in an ecstatic, trance state as outlined above.

In addition to this, many shamans adopt animal totems, and wear ritual gear symbolic of this relationship. It is thought that wearing special costuming helps to facilitate movement between the material and spiritual realms by removing the shaman from familiarity. Such costuming may simply be a mask or head-dress, or may be as elaborate as an entire body suit.

Finally, Eliade points out that no shaman can be identified as such without recognition from their respective communities. The shaman is intermediary between the sacred and the profane, and as such acts on behalf the tribe rather than merely for selfish gain.

If correlations for each of these identifiers can be found in Celtic material (through the vernacular literature, the archaeological record and through later folk traditions) then one would be justified in assuming that shamanistic practice is in evidence. In this sense, I intend to follow the maxim: *If they look like shamans, and they act like shamans, then they probably are shamans.*

o0o

Investigating the survival of primal Celtic shamanism in later folk traditions will necessitate a broad view of Celtic culture, drawing from many tribal sources throughout the Celtic world and invoking cultural comparisons from classically recognised shamanic practices. Having established the nature of tribal Celtic shamanism, we can then look at the physical appearance of the Celtic shaman as recorded by history (drawing largely on literary sources, supported by the archaeological record): Part One.

With this in mind, the next stage is to identify the ecstatic and shamanic elements in ritual and establish whether or not these may be considered 'authentic'. This will involve a closer look at the trance phenomena, and how it was achieved: Part Two.

Finally, the Gaelic oral tradition as preserved in the late nineteenth and early twentieth centuries must be scrutinised in order to draw attention to any instances of shamanistic practice and awareness it may demonstrate: Part Three.

Whilst we may use intercultural comparisons to establish the authenticity of Celtic shamanism, it is important to keep in mind that each culture is distinct and unique, and so it will not be possible to attach Celtic shamanism to any homogenous definition. Instead, it is my aim to show that the Celts evolved their own techniques for coming into a personal and interactive union with the Sacred, techniques which were born from the individuality of their own culture.

Interpretation is a flawed process, constrained by the shackles of human prejudices and subjectivity: as Nietzsche says 'there are no facts, only interpretations'. A 'close reading' can often lead to the imposition of a certain point of view – even when such a view is not fully supported by the available evidence. There is a traditional Haitian Vodou proverb: 'when the anthropologists arrive, the gods leave the island'.[16] In this study, I hope to remain true to the Celtic spirit, and not cast the gods of our ancestors into exile.

PART ONE

DRUIDS AND DRUMS:
THE INSTRUMENTS OF ECSTASY

His caftan is made of a goat or reindeer skin. A quantity of ribbon kerchiefs sewn to its frock represent snakes, some of them being shaped into snakes' heads with two eyes and open jaws. The tails of the larger snakes have only one head… There are also a number of iron objects, among them a miniature bow and arrows, to frighten the spirits. On the back of the shirt are sewn animal pelts and two copper disks. The collar is decorated with a fringe of black and brown owl feathers.

Mircea Eliade - *Shamanism: Archaic Techniques of Ecstasy*

Laying the Foundation Stone

T'aint no sin to take off your skin, and dance around in your bones.

Tom Waits

The word druid comes from the Old Irish word *druad*. Its meaning is the subject of some controversy, having many false or poorly fitting etymologies forced upon it. The proto-Celtic languages grew out of Indo-European roots, so it is here we must turn in order to discover its meaning.

Pliny gave the origin of the 'dru' part as a derivative of the Greek *drus*, meaning an oak tree. This may be correct, as it is connected to an old Indo-European word with the same meaning. In addition, 'dru' may also derive from an Indo-European root word meaning strong – the same root which gives the English word 'true'.

The second element (*wid-) is connected to the same root word which gives rise to the English word 'witness'. It relates to knowledge of things which are personally experienced.[1]

From both of these elements, a more general meaning emerges. One interpretation could be one who has 'enduring knowledge' which is personally experienced. Here we find a relationship with the word *druad* and the word *šaman*, in that both relate to experiential wisdom.

An alternative interpretation reveals further shamanic connotations. One who has 'knowledge of the oak' is reminiscent of the 'world tree' employed by many shamanic cultures to transcend the ordinary material realm. Pliny the Elder's *Natural History* reports that the druids have a special affinity for the oak tree, apparently revering it above any other.[2]

Taking all of these possibilities into account perhaps gives a more rounded view on the meaning of *druad*. The oak tree is often perceived across cultural boundaries as the 'strong tree'. This places the emphasis on the enduring nature of the druid's knowledge, knowledge which was gained through a *personal interaction* with *natural forces*: that is, a shamanistic interaction through animistic means.

oOo

To begin to see the evidence for Celtic shamanism, one must first be prepared to look at the material through an intercultural lens. By doing so, it is possible to enhance what we already know of primal Celtic culture and its later descendants; viewing the sources shamanistically, in some cases, provides us with the only plausible explanation for otherwise inexplicable references.

We can see evidence for this in the tale Aithed Muirne re Dubh Ruis.[3] In this tale, through the emotional trauma of seeing her father killed in battle, Mis is driven mad. Upon seeing his bleeding body on the battlefield, Mis sucks the blood from his wounds (*...iar bhfaghāil an* [51] *chuirp go n-iomad créachta di, gabhus ag súgha 7 ag ól na fola as na crēachtuibh.*) Mis retreats from civilisation, living in the mountains and forests, and grows a *clúmh* (from the Latin *pluma*, meaning 'feathers'). She becomes a cannibal, her taste for human flesh becoming so voracious as to have caused the Barony of Clan Maurice to become like a desert.[4]

Trevarthen first made the comparison between Mis and the Kwakiutl hamatsa shaman.[5] The hamatsa is a cannibal dancer and must be returned to civilisation by their community after periods of ecstatic cannibalism. Mis' return from her *geltacht* (madness) is also compared by Trevarthen to the hamatsa's. Both are bathed ritually to wash off the stain of wildness (in which Mis loses her feather coat) and made to eat a civilised meal. Both undergo a lengthy re-education process (in the case of the hamatsa, this can last from 1 – 3 years[6]).

There are a great deal of parallels between Celtic shamanism and that found in Kwakiutl culture. We can begin to see the similarities when we compare the image of a hamatsa cannibal dancer with images taken from the Gundestrup cauldron (see

4

below). The postures depicted in these examples of Celtic iconography also reflect a later Christian prayer stance, known as orans posture. This method of prayer is deemed to be more 'interactive' than supplicatory, again suggesting a shamanic origin for the practice. Unfortunately our evidence for both cultures does not allow us to delve deeper into their respective similarities, making this comparison merely speculative. I include it here for the sake of completeness.

Kwakiutl *hamatsa* cannibal dancer

Plates c and a of the Gundestrup Cauldron

Whilst the cultural comparisons in this tale point towards a shamanic interpretation, the most convincing argument comes from the king of Munster's proclamation that Mis is to be returned to society unharmed. The usual punishment for her crimes would have been death, but the king of Munster offers a substantial reward for her capture alive. On the surface, this appears to make no sense. Viewed shamanistically, however, we may begin to bring it into focus. If the king recognised a more spiritual aspect to Mis' *geltacht*, his decision would begin to make sense. Shamans traditionally are of great value to their community, and it would therefore stand to reason that Mis should not be harmed.

We can see this theme recurring in other, more easily recognised, Celtic tales. In *Serglige Con Culainn*, when Cú Chulainn's men wish to try and rouse him from his wasting sickness, Fergus recognises the importance of his experience and advises them not to do so, as he is receiving a vision.[7]

The value of re-examining the source material from a shamanistic perspective therefore is obvious, and yields some very worthwhile interpretations. In so doing, we are able to place Celtic shamanism within a broader category of visionary experience.

oOo

Celticists and archaeologists were not the first to recognise shamanistic elements in primal Celtic culture – certain contemporary classical commentators pre-empted this theory, although they lacked the correct language with which to frame their observations. One enlightening report comes from Tacitus' *Germania* in relation to the perception of deity.

> They do not, however, deem it consistent with the divine majesty to imprison their gods within walls, *or to represent them with anything like human features*. Their holy places are the woods and groves, and they call by the name of god that hidden presence which is *only seen by the eye of reverence*.[8]

'They' in this account refers to one Germanic tribe, however in classical texts Germanic and Celtic tribes often become confused, and it is entirely plausible that Tacitus may have done so too. Moreover, Celtic and Germanic tribes were geographical neighbours, and would probably have shared certain cultural, linguistic and spiritual similarities. All of the above denies the possibility of discounting the above description, as its implications on the Celts are clear.

Tacitus states that the tribal gods are worshipped outdoors, and are not anthropomorphised. This complements an animistic philosophy – since spirit and divinity is omnipresent, there is no need to build temples or churches. Another important factor which Tacitus notes is that these spirits and deities can only be seen by 'the eye of reverence'. The direct perception of deity through contemplative means is a shamanistic practice – regardless of whether or not such 'contemplative means' include trance.

The cultural bias of Greek and Roman commentators places a restriction on their reports of primal Celtic culture. Since neither the Greeks nor the Romans came into contact with any traditional shamanic cultures, they lack the necessary vocabulary to describe it. For this reason, Tacitus' explanation of Germanic (and possibly Celtic) spirituality is vague and enigmatic.

The use of classical commentaries as a source on primal Celtic culture, then, must be balanced against this restriction. Moreover, the cultural bias of Greek and Roman writers would prevent an accurate description of 'foreign' customs and practices. It is important to remember, for example, that Caesar was writing in order to support imperialist propaganda and personal interest. We can see, in the language Caesar uses to describe the Celts, that he is keen to promote the 'noble savage' image – both to dehumanise his enemies, and also to heighten the importance of his victories in Gaul.

Despite these cautionary notes, the classical writers remain one of our best sources of information on primal Celtic culture. They are our only contemporary account, and as such cannot be ignored.

We face a similar dilemma with the earliest written native accounts. All surviving accounts in Old Irish were written down in the Christian period, when many pagan or shamanic elements may have been deemed heretical or distasteful, and therefore 'edited' out. In these cases, a close reading of each text is essential in order to expunge what may be later additions.

There are a number of examples which point toward continuity with pagan spirituality in the vernacular literature. To take one at random, many Old Irish tales speak of Goibnhiu (Gofannon in Welsh tales), a smith/god character. This name is probably cognate with the Gaulish deity Gobanus, worshipped in Switzerland, and found on local inscriptions as Gobanus Dobnoredus or 'he who rules the earth'.[9]

However, another problem faced in examining the literature comes from issues of translation. Many of the tales which survive were translated into English in a time when a shamanistic hypothesis would have been unthinkable. To this end, shamanic material may have either been badly translated, or missed out entirely. As a result it has proven necessary to return to some texts in their original and offer a more reasonable and supportive translation.

Finally, the archaeological record provides some valuable clues on how animals were used to compliment the animistic world-view of many Celtic tribes. Iconography and artefacts, together with physical remains found in ritually significant sites, all provide useful information on how shamanistic practice was implemented in ancient times. It is important to remember, however, that archaeology is a subjective science, and any one interpretation may be counterbalanced by an equally plausible and contradictory interpretation.

Am torc ar gáill...

In all classically shamanic cultures, shamans carry a number of accessories which characterise their responsibilities within the community. These accessories include shamanic instruments and ritual costuming which constitute a religious cosmography and hierophany which discloses not only the presence of the Sacred, but also reveals the metaphysic behind the society it supports.

> The costume represents a religious microcosm qualitatively different from the surrounding profane space. For one thing, it constitutes an almost complete symbolic system; for another, its consecration has impregnated it with various spiritual forces and especially with 'spirits'. By the mere fact of donning it – or manipulating the objects that deputize for it – the shaman transcends profane space and prepares to enter into contact with the spiritual world.[10]

Magical objects and tools form a part of the shamanic costume, and in some cultures replace it entirely. In either case, the shaman often possesses a number of ritual items which facilitate their journey into the spirit world and provide a focus for manifesting their spiritual power within the physical world.

From a purely psychological perspective, the appearance of the shaman may contribute to their status within the community. Animal symbology not only demonstrates the shaman's power over a particular creature, for example, but also crystallises an absorption of that animal's attributes into themselves. Therefore, by appearance alone, the shaman may show that they have the strength of a bear, or the cunning of the wolf, just to give two common examples.

Recent surveys reveal that roughly eighty percent of all communication is non-verbal. Excluding any extra-sensory abilities, the vast majority of information conveyed from one person to another is visual. This reinforces the importance of the shaman's costuming and instruments not only for the spiritual assistance they provide the practitioner, but also for the status it gives compared to the rest of the community.

> The shaman's costume and implements make the spiritual reality he experiences visible to all who see him. Physical objects used in the shaman's work act as tangible representations of their other world helpers. As physical transitional objects, they also help invoke their spiritual counterparts, bridging the gap between the worlds.[11]

The concept of the shaman's instruments as 'transitional objects' was first put forward by British psychologist D. W. Winnicott. Winnicott explains that these objects may be either psychological or physical, and can range from something as simple as a child's teddy bear, to as sophisticated as the shaman's spirit totem.

Such transitional objects support a person who is holding what Winnicott describes as 'transitional space'; a state of consciousness in which psychological change can occur. In this state, one is not locked into habitual mindsets – a state of consciousness which is not at too far remove from that achieved by the shaman in trance journeys to the spirit world.

If this is true, then we can begin to understand why the shaman needs his various accoutrements; both to assist in holding a 'transitional' trance state; and to visually communicate his status and powers to onlookers during ritual. The costume and instruments of the shaman, therefore, both represent and facilitate their ability to interact with the spirits.

o0o

Whilst it is acknowledged that all cultures are measured by their individualities, there are a number of recurring images common throughout shamanic cultures which we can use as a yardstick for purposes of comparison. Perhaps the greatest and most obvious example of these is the use of avian symbology in shamanic costuming.

> The shamanic costume tends to give the shaman a new, magical body in animal form. The three chief types are that of the bird, the reindeer (or stag), and the bear – but especially the bird.[12]

Examples of these are ubiquitous. The Manchu shaman, whose spirituality and practices have been influenced by successive waves of Sino-Buddhist culture, wear headgear that is made from feathers and represents a bird. The Mongol shaman wears bird wings on his shoulders and 'feels that he is changed into a bird'[13] when he wears them. Among the Altaians, Eliade speculates that ornithomorphic appearance was more accentuated in earlier times. Today, however, only owl feathers are used in shamanic decoration.

It is fair to say that bird costuming is often seen as indispensable in order to make the flight to the spirit world. Aerial symbolism and references to flight are found throughout the shamanic world: as flight capable animals birds are the perfect representation of the spirit flight (*aithed* in Old Irish). In addition to birds, Eliade mentions the stag and the bear as two other commonly recurring animals in shamanic costuming, and we can see all three used in Celtic shamanism.

In addition, we see the use of masks and drums as the most common magical implements in shamanic cultures. The use of masks in ritual visually represent trance possession. In the Tungus tradition, an improvised mask is created for the shaman in order 'to show that the spirit of *malu* is in him'.[14] In other traditions the mask is used by the shaman as a disguise in front of the spirits. In the Altai and among the Goldi, when the shaman leads a dead person's soul to the spirit world, he daubs his face with suet for this purpose.[15]

Of all the shaman's instruments the drum is of primary importance. It is the crux of the shamanic séance, helping to summon the spirits into physical ritual space.

> The drumming at the beginning of the séance, intended to summon the spirits and 'shut them up' in the shaman's drum, constitutes the preliminaries for the ecstatic journey.[16]

The drum enables the shaman to make the spirit journey, and conversely, can be used to allow the shaman to focus again on the physical world after their journey (by changing the rhythm of the beat, thus interrupting trance). For whatever purpose it is used, it appears a widespread instrument for engaging in shamanic activities.

By taking these commonalities and holding them up against Celtic culture, we are able to locate the shamanism buried not too far beneath its surface. Whilst it is important to remember that differences will be apparent from natural cultural diversity, I believe that it is possible to demonstrate that primal Celtic shamanism employed all of the above costumes and instruments in their rituals, and many others besides. The archaeological record and classical sources provide most of our information for this, however there are some Old Irish texts which demonstrate shamanic costuming and paraphernalia.

o0o

Forbhais Droma Dámhgháire, on which much of the literary evidence of this section is based, can only be found in the *Book of Lismore*. A valuable collection of manuscripts in its own right, the *Book of Lismore* dates from around the fifteenth century. We know, through references in the *Book of Leinster*, however, that this particular tale is much older, dating at least from the twelfth century, but possibly as early as the third.[17]

The story concerns the march of high-king Cormac Mac Airt, his army and his druids, from Tara to Munster in order to compel the latter to pay tribute to them. Through many battles, Cormac's forces appear to gain the upper hand. This is not attributed to their military prowess, however, but through the superior magic of their druids. Fiacha Moilleathan, king of South Munster, becomes desperate as Cormac's druids dry up all the wells and reduce his army to 'shadows'.

In this extremity, Fiacha applies to the renowned Munster druid Mogh Roith. He agrees to help them and restores the water supply. Then, through a series of transformations and by means of a magical druid fire, Mogh Roith succeeds in driving Cormac's army out of Munster.

Very rarely in the vernacular sources do we find descriptions of the druids themselves; this is why *Forbhais Droma Dámhgháire* is so important for the purposes of this study. Mogh Roith's ritual gear and instruments are illustrated in detail, as well as how they are used. As one of the only sources to give this information, we can only assume that it is not atypical, and that depictions of druids therein would be acceptable to contemporary readers. Despite this however, the introduction to Sean Ó Duinn's translation has this to say:

> The practice of magic plays a highly significant role in this story and the two groups associated with the magic arts – the Druids and the Aos Sí or Tuatha Dé Dannan, are not as clearly distinguished from each other as they are in other texts.[18]

This lack of clarity between the druids and the spirits is significant, as the shaman is able to move freely between the material and the spiritual, making them almost indistinguishable with the spirits themselves. This may also point to the druid's ability to cross the boundaries between physical reality and spiritual reality at will. Ó Duinn continues:

[*Forbhais Droma Dámhgháire*] is a storehouse of ancient tradition, a story of land-divisions and tribal origins, of kings and heroes, of the rule of law and precedent and above all a tale of mystery and magic in which the otherworldly powers of the sí invade the world of men.[19]

The ancient traditions as they are presented in the text are significant to our journey into primal Celtic spirituality. They reveal a shamanistic mode of practice not at all consistent with modern interpretations of other Irish epics. This provides a strong shamanic foundation for the interaction between spiritual and physical realities so often present in Celtic literature.

Certain analyses of this text have necessitated close scrutiny of the text in its original language. In such cases, as with selections below from *Aithed Muirne re Dubh Ruis*, I have provided quotations of the English and the original side by side. I believe these translations to be more accurate, as well as more sympathetic to a 'corrected' view of primal Celtic shamanism.

In Flight to the Spirits

The *gelta* – those undergoing a physically induced psycho-spiritual trauma not dissimilar to the initiatory sickness which 'calls' many shamans to their vocations – often wore feather dress. We can see this in *Aithed Muirne re Dubh Ruis*: when Mis withdraws from civilised life she grows a *clúmh*, or feathered covering. In *Buile Suibhne* ('The Frenzy of Suibhne'), we see the same description. Both Mis and Suibhne are *geltacht*, a quality akin to madness or frenzy, which may be indicative of an ecstatic awareness. Some scholars have gone as far as to suggest that Suibhne, and all *gelta* by extension, were 'possessed by and possessors of supernatural inspiration and power, a practitioner of archaic techniques of ecstasy'.[20]

Mis's *clúmh* enables her to levitate and travel 'like the wind' – possibly metaphors for the spirit flight:

> *Do chuir fós foluamhain a gealtachais an seoladh*
> *siubhail sin fúithe go ritheach mar na ngaoith ionas go*
> *sáruigheadh a rith, nídh ar bith budh mhian lē...*

> Moreover, the flightiness of her madness gave her such
> an impetus that she would run like the wind, so that she
> would overtake anything she wanted to in the world.[21]

She uses these abilities in her state of *geltacht* to consume the flesh and blood of her victims, absorbing their spiritual energies into herself.

We know that such associations with bird dress are not unique just to the *gelta* however. The *filid* are recorded as having worn *tuigen*, which were elaborate bird-feather capes. *Tuigen* means 'bird covering',[22] and its shamanic associations have been noted:

> The same symbolism of the sacred costume survives in
> more developed religions: wolf or bear furs in China, the
> bird feathers of the Irish prophet, and so on. We find the
> macrocosmic symbolism on the robes of the priests and
> sovereigns of the ancient Orient. This series of facts falls
> under a 'law' well known to the history of religions: *one*
> *becomes what one displays.*[23]

Cormac's glossary describes the *tuigen* in more detail. It was made from the skins of white and multi-coloured birds from the girdle down. From the girdle upwards to the neck, it was adorned with mallard's necks and crests.[24]

We can assume from these analyses that the associations behind the *tuigen* were probably totemic. This identification is made manifest in a number of tales, in one example an interloper amongst a group of bird caped *filid* is described as not 'a bird fit for their flock'.[25] This blurring of language and adoption of animal identity is a common feature in shamanic cultures where the shaman becomes indistinct from the spirits and their totems.

Among the Borneo tribe of the Iban, birds are thought to serve as a link between the living and the spirits of the ancestors.[26] This is a concept which translates easily into Celtic culture, which the archaeological record appears to suggest. Skeletons of ravens and crows have been found in dried up wells and pits, the significance of which seems to be sacrificial. At the Iron Age fort of Winklebury, a pit was found containing a pig burial with a spread-winged raven beneath.[27] In addition, a great number of ravens occur in the Danebury pits, apparently forming the focus of a special ritual in this location.[28] Green argues that:

> Ravens my have been associated with pits and wells because of a perceived chthonic symbolism: ritual shafts penetrate deep underground, forming a line of communication between the living and the dead, the earth and the underworld powers. Ravens and crows, with their black plumage and their habit of feeding off dead things, were clearly seen as messengers from the Otherworld.[29]

Irish mythology supports this supposition. Badh Catha, goddess of death and battle, whose name actually means 'battle crow', was often represented by the raven, as was the Mórrighan, goddess of oracles and death. This notion survives into modern Gaelic: *fitheach*, meaning 'raven', literally means 'omen bird' or 'bird of augury'.

Diodorus Siculus refers to the wearing of animal crested helmets by the Celts.[30] Such helmets are known archaeologically, and are thought to have had a totemic, shamanistic effect on the wearer's psyche. The association with the goddess of battle, together with her animal spirit representative, would aid the warrior's spiritual battle powers –

as we shall see in the example of Mogh Roith below, the warrior shaman is a recurring theme in Celtic literature.

A Celtic helmet dating from around the third century BCE was found in Ciumesti in Romania with the figure of a raven on top. This piece is especially interesting because the wings are hinged in such a way so that when its wearer ran towards their enemy, the raven's wings would flap up and down in imitation of flight. This compares to images of Celtic warriors[31] on the Gundestrup cauldron wearing helmets with feathered and antlered crests below.

Ciumesti Celtic Helmet

Plate E of the Gundestrup Cauldron

In addition to these, a curious depiction on an Etruscan pot at Citta della Pierce shows an image of a Celtic warrior being attacked by a raven. The raven is pecking his eye – significant in a shamanic context as blindness in one eye is a theme which has travelled the millennia from ancient to modern practice. For more on this particular theme, see section three: *A Shaman in the Gàidhealtachd.*

Ravens and crows, however, were not the only birds significant to the Celts. Fionn MacCumhaill is represented in the literature as custodian of Mannanan Mac Lir's crane bag – a bag of inspirational treasures with their own shamanistic significance. According to Giraldus Cambrensis, there was a taboo on eating cranes in Ireland, perhaps an association with this tale. Swans, chickens and geese are also significant birds archaeologically, linked with rituals of death or as offerings to local deities.[32]

Each of these birds has individual significance in classically shamanic cultures. For example, the chicken is a pivotal animal in the healing rituals of the Sea Dyak shaman or *manang.* Swans are of great importance to Samoyed, Siberian, Altaian and Lapp shamans, amongst others. The goose, to the Altaic shaman, is often a spiritual substitute for the horse: we see a number of myths where the ecstatic returns from the spirit world riding on its back.[33]

However, perhaps most significantly for our study, is the practical application of avian symbolism in druidic costuming as presented in the tale *Forbhais Droma Dámhgháire.* Here we see not only what kind of ritual costuming Mogh Roith possessed, but also how it was used to shamanic effect.

Towards the end of the tale Mogh Roith uses a magical druid fire in order to defeat Cormac Mac Airt's army. When the fires are lit and enchanted, he calls for his shamanic equipment.

Tugadh ansin a sheithe thairbh mhaoil odhair go Mogh Roith chomh maith lena éanchealtair alabhreac lena heití foluaineacha agus an chuid eile dá threalamh draíochta.
D' imigh sé leis suas san aer agus san fhirmimint ansin in éineacht leis an tine agus bhí sé ag casadh agus

ag bualadh na tine ar a dhícheall agus reitric á reacairacht aige: 'Deilbhim saigheada druadh...'

The bull-hide from a horn-less brown bull belonging to Mogh Roith was now brought to him along with his speckled bird-mask with its billowing wings and the rest of his druidic gear.
   He proceeded to fly up into the sky and the firmament along with the fire, and he continued to turn and beat the fire towards the north as he chanted a rhetoric: 'I fashion druid's arrows...'[34]

This is clearly shamanism in action. The text specifically states that the *éanchealtair*, translated here as 'speckled bird-mask', was brought to Mogh Roith in order to help him 'fly up into the sky and the firmament along with the fire'. As mentioned previously, masks are of particular significance amongst classically shamanic cultures. *'One becomes what one displays...'* therefore Mogh Roith is able to assume the power of flight by wearing a bird-mask.

The word *éanchealtair* is composed of two elements: *éan*, which signifies its avian connotations; and *cealtair*. The Old Irish word *celtar* means 'cloak' or 'covering', which may point towards Mogh Roith's wearing a *tuigen*. However, a second version of this text has *eanceannch* instead of *éanchealtair* – which would be more correctly translated as 'feathered head-dress'. In any of the above cases, we can see one common ground – that Mogh Roith puts on bird costuming in order to fly up with the druid fire and direct its course. There can be no ambiguity in the interpretation of this part of the tale; and there are no end of cultural comparisons amongst classically shamanic cultures. The Marind shaman

...goes to a sort of lodge that he has built in the forest from palm leaves, and equips his upper arms and forearms with long plumes from a heron. Finally, he sets fire to his hut, without leaving it ... the smoke and flames are to lift him into the air, and, like a bird, he flies where he will...[35]

In the rituals of the Kwakiutl *hamatsa* (a culture very close to primal Celtic culture), we may also find a further parallel.[36] During a ceremony known as *kwakwaka'wakw* the sacred dancer wears a raven's mask. This facilitates the dancer's transformation into the raven itself during the ritual. At the end of the ceremony, the mask is opened to reveal a painted human face inside, thus completing the transformation full circle again.[37]

> ...the mask manifestly announces the incarnation of a mythical personage (ancestor, mythical animal, god). For its part, the costume transubstantiates the shaman, it transforms him, before all eyes, into a superhuman being. And this is equally true whether the predominant attribute that it seeks to display is the prestige of a dead man returned to life (skeleton) or ability to fly (bird), or the condition of husband to a 'celestial spouse' (women's dress, feminine attributes), and so forth.[38]

The mask in ritual, then, both implies the capabilities of the creature being assumed, and also raises the prestige of the wearer to a supernatural level. Mogh Roith, in wearing an *éanchealtair* during ecstatic ritual, imbues himself with the ability to fly, and increases his own power in order to better defeat the opposing armies.

The second paragraph from *Forbhais Droma Dámhgháire* cited earlier implies the use of chant in order for Mogh Roith to make his ecstatic journey: 'as he chanted a rhetoric'. This technique to enter trance and the spirit flight will be discussed in greater detail in the second section, however it is important to note its significance here. It implies that Mogh Roith's flight is spiritual, and not a physical travelling upwards with the flames. His attack against Cormac Mac Airt's army is a spiritual one, on a shamanic level of consciousness. No text in the Old Irish canon more clearly displays the use of shamanic costuming and the spirit journey.

oOo

Bird imagery aside, we are also confronted with more animal costuming in this Old Irish passage. Before calling for his *éanchealtair*, Mogh Roith is brought his bull-hide. This reinforces the conclusion that Mogh Roith's flight is spiritual rather than physical, as bull's hides are often used in Celtic traditions as a wrapping to restrict movement during trance. Sensory deprivation techniques are common in almost all shamanic cultures, and are a significant feature of initiatory ordeals.

Among Australian shamans, the chosen initiate is carried to a cemetery and left there 'bound, for several nights'.[39] A Palaeolithic image from Sicily shows a number of initiates bound with their limbs behind them. They are surrounded by figures in bird masks – a scene which has often been interpreted as a sacrifice, although the latter do not appear to be harming the bound figures.[40] The method of binding all limbs together behind the back is used by Inuit shamans for the purposes of prophecy and trance possession.[41]

The psychology behind wrapping or binding appears to be to allow the mental faculties to go into overdrive. When physical sensation is taken away from the neophyte or the shaman proper, they are more fully able to experience the spiritual aspect of reality – as one kind of sensation grows dim, the other is brightened. The universality of this practice appears to point towards a common use in shamanic cultures, and Celtic culture is no exception.

Ceangal nan tri chaol, or the 'binding of the three narrows' is an intriguing practice which appears in various Old Irish and Scots Gaelic sources.[42] The origins of the term are uncertain, however it appears to describe the process of binding the 'wrists, ankles and waist [or neck]'[43] with all three fastened behind the back. The shaman in the Lakota Yuwipi ceremony is similarly bound. A modern account describes this in detail.

> Horn Cloud took a short thong [and] began to tie ... Plenty Wolf's hands together. He then placed the quilt over Plenty Wolf's head so that one corner completely hooded his face ... Horn Cloud took from his pocket a long leather thong, one end of which had already been fastened into a slipknot, and placed it over Plenty Wolf's head, securing it tightly over his quilt covered neck...[44]

The ceremony continues as the quilt is secured around Plenty Wolf, the thong wrapped around his body, tied behind his back and finally secured around his ankles. Plenty Wolf was then able to speak to his spirits in the darkness, and invoked their aid for the purposes of the ceremony. One idea for binding in this situation is that the pathetic state of the shaman moves the spirits to act in his aid.

Ceangal nan tri chaol is both painful and undignified. The king of Lochlan is described as having endured this process. He was 'thrown to the ground on the heath, in front of everybody and subjected to the tying up of the 3 thin sprouts (it was not an honour for a king!) / *am fiadhnuis chàich air an fraoch, / Dho-sa, 's cha b'onair righ, / Chuirt' air ceangal nan tri chaol* [45]

Perhaps the most famous and well attested visionary practice involving binding or wrapping in Celtic history is the *tarbfeis*. Archaeology confirms that the bull was revered:

> Gaulish and British sanctuaries show evidence of ritual involving cattle: at Digeon (Somme) oxen formed important offerings; and at Mirebeau (Côte d'Or), young cattle (between 2 and 4 years old) were killed and eaten in cult banquets ... In Britian, several shrines show signs of cattle sacrifice and ritual: outside a rectangular shrine at South Cadbury Castle, an adult cow was buried; another small sanctuary at the site was associated with six pits containing horse and cattle skulls. A third sacred

building was approached by an avenue of pit-burials of young animals, including calves … A complete bull was interred along with other beasts at the subterranean Cambridge shrine.[46]

This reverence is also shown by the use of the bull's hide in other ritual and visionary practices. Medh and Aillil's druid, MacRoth, wears a bull's hide on his journey to survey the enemy troops in the *Táin Bó Cúailnge.*

In the *tarbfeis* a bull was sacrificed and a person wrapped in its hide. As others chanted, he or she received the answer to a question previously posed to the spirits. The *Serglige Con Culainn* describes this practice in a section relating to the election of kings.[47] The shamanic significance of being wrapped in a bull's hide is not new to Celtic scholarship. Stuart Piggot highlights its use, citing Siberian parallels:

…the bull's hide was employed in ritual divination, much as the Yakut shaman sat in ecstasy on his mare's skin invoking the 'mighty bull of the earth' and the 'horse of the steppe' … Nor were such rites confined to Medieval Ireland, for the 11th century Burchard of Worms enjoins the priest to enquire of the potentially sinful member of his flock whether, at the Kalends of January, he had sat on a bull's hide at a crossroad, thinking thereby to know the future … Celtic seer and Siberian shaman had much in common.[48]

A bull's hide would certainly be big enough to cover the practitioner fully, blocking out all light. This would allow them to 'see' more clearly the spiritual aspect of reality. It is perhaps this spiritual brightness which is being invoked by Mogh Roith in the druid fire ceremony.

Physical darkness and restriction of movement is a sensory deprivation method which we see again in the later hagiographies of Celtic saints. Perhaps a memory of the *tarbfeis* led them to their practices, an echo of both primal and pagan

Celtic ecstasy.[49] Perhaps a culture which fostered direct, visionary perception of the Sacred could not be completely eradicated by the proselytising of later religious movements.

oOo

Many Celticists and archaeologists alike have been haunted by the image of the horned character depicted on the Gundestrup cauldron. It appears, certainly at first glace, to be the perfect iconographical representation of the shaman: the figure wears a horned head-dress, is sitting in a trance posture, and is surrounded by images of animals (possibly a portrayal of the spirit journey, or simply representative of the close relationship the shaman shares with the natural world). This image is often married to Romano-Celtic images of the horned god of the Celts, Cernunnos, or 'horned one'.

Plate A of the Gundestrup Cauldron

Gaulish 'Cernunos'

The significant of horns or antlers to the shaman has been widely commented upon. Antlers are common features of Turkish and Korean shamans. In addition, 'the cult of the stag is typical of hunter and nomad cultures, in which shamanesses do not appear to play much of a role'.[50] Thus antlers or other stag imagery appears to be the preserve of male shamans only. The Tungusic shaman's costume represents a stag, whose skeleton is suggested by pieces of iron. Its antlers are also made of iron, transforming the shaman into the animal itself.[51]

We see evidence for this transformation in Celtic literature also. In the Fionn Cycle, Fionn's wife Sabha is represented as part deer, part human. The first time Fionn meets her, she is in the shape of a fawn, having been transformed by the magic of a druid. Her son, Oisin (whose name means 'little deer') is perceived as having a special affinity with stags, and is sometimes described as half-fawn himself.[52] In another tale of this cycle, a woman from the spirit world is sent to lure Fionn to the domain of the god Donn mac Midir in the form of a fawn. In a second version of this tale, it is the god Donn himself who transforms into a stag by means of his own magic.

In shamanic cultures, the shaman physically 'becomes' the animal displayed through his costuming. If this is so, then the depictions above may not represent actual shapeshifting, but rather shamanic costuming, allowing the wearer to enter the psyche of the animal he or she dons.

This interpretation appears to be more consistent with the 'mood' of the imagery presented on the Gundestrup cauldron. The animals surrounding the central shaman may simply represent animals (reinforcing the animistic and totemic functions of the shaman); but conversely may represent a shamanic 'trance dance' ritual. The surrounding figures may also represent shamans in full animal costuming, 'dancing' the spirit of the animals they represent.

25

> Dancing, accompanied by drumming, is the far more
> common method employed by shamans throughout
> much of the primitive world to achieve a shamanic state
> of consciousness sufficient to having the experience.
> The initiation of shamans among the Carib Indians of
> northern South America, for example, involves
> nighttime dancing during which the neophytes move in
> imitation of animals. This is part of a process of learning
> how to turn into animals.[53]

Dancing in order to transform into an animal is not restricted to
shamanic cultures alone however. In many primal cultures,
anyone with a guardian spirit may use dancing as a means of
evoking his alter ego. Among the Coast Salish Indians of the
Northwest Coast, the winter dance season provides an
opportunity for the individual to consciously unite with the
spirit of their individual power animals.

> The dancer's spirit finds its dramatized expression in
> dance steps, tempo, movements, miens and gestures: in
> the sneaking pace, then flying leaps of the ferociously
> yelling 'warrior', or in the swaying trot of the plump,
> sadly weeping 'bear mother'; in the rubber-like reptilian
> writhing of the 'double headed serpent' ... in the 'lizard'
> who sheds tears over his devoured offspring or in the
> mighty 'whale' who grabs smaller fish.[54]

Much animalesque dancing in primal cultures has as its
objective the unification of spirit animals with the dancers,
whether or not the rituals are purely shamanic in other respects.
Thus the dance of the Beast Gods by the Zuni Pueblo in the
American Southwest bears a strong resemblance to shamanic
séances among other cultures. Such rituals take animal imitation
one step beyond, to spiritual union with the animal itself.

In the case of Mogh Roith, we can see this intention clearly.
Wrapped in a bull's hide, wearing feathered costuming,
chanting, he is able to take on the spirit of the bird his costume
deputises for and fly up the flames of his spiritual fire. Michael

Harner, a well respected modern shamanic practitioner of western extraction, has stipulated that drumming in the above context also aids the shaman in his spirit journeys. It is now to this element of shamanic instrumentation that we shall turn our attention.

Reinventing the Wheel

Drumming is a crucial technique to most shamanic cultures, a catalyst for the spirit journey. This is not to say, however, that without the drum a culture cannot be considered shamanic. The Inuit shaman, in contrast to North Asian and other shamanic groups, lacks both the ritual costume proper, and the drum.[55] This does not have the effect of 'clipping the shamans wings' however, as the *angakok* undertakes frequent ecstatic journeys to the sky (to contact the *Sila*) or the depths of the sea (to approach *Takánakapsâluk*, the Mother of the Sea Beasts). The Eskimo shaman is a 'specialist in magical flight. Some shamans have visited the moon, others have flown around the earth. According to the traditions, shamans fly like birds, spreading their arms as a bird does its wings'.[56]

As an ecstatic technique, we do not see many references to drumming in the vernacular sources. Other kinds of music and chant often appear to take precedence, however this does not necessarily exclude the drum from Celtic shamanism. Trevarthen notes:

> Drums are simple instruments. Each baby invents the drum on its own, banging something against something else. Therefore, it is hard to imagine the Celts did not use them.[57]

In addition to this, Kopp argues that a child will develop this impulse around the age of seven months, and identifies the

27

'drumming instinct' as one of the earliest stages in infant development.[58]

The archaeological record cannot help us in our search for the origins of the drum in the British Isles or Ireland, as drums are made of perishable materials and have not survived. However, it has been acknowledged that 'any pot covered with skin tightened down to protect its contents is a potential drum'.[59] Some clues may survive in the iconography, however, which might help to point us on our way.

The circular, spoked objects often represented in early Celtic art are hard to explain. Many appear to be chariot wheels, but taken completely out of context. For example, many early Celtic artworks show the wheel being carried by an individual in what appears to be a processional, religious context. This has led many scholars to conclude that the spoked circle is a solar symbol – which may be the case, but only represents one point of view.

It is possible, given the context of such images (like those from the Gundestrup cauldron below), that these may represent frame drums. They certainly appear to be carried by prominent individuals at the head of processions – a place of honour which may have been reserved for the shaman.

Plate C of the Gundestrup Cauldron

28

Close-up of plate C

The fact that this possible drum is represented as a wheel may be a deliberate double meaning which points to shamanic conventions regarding their instruments. (For a comparison with the above 'frame drum' image and a shamanic drum, see the image of a Mongolian Shaman, *Otsir Böö*, at the end of the next chapter). The drum, as the vehicle for the shamanic journey, is often represented as a horse or similar mode of transportation.

> The drumming at the beginning of the séance … constitutes the preliminaries for the ecstatic journey. This is why the drum is called the 'shaman's horse' (Yakut, Buryat). The Altaic drum bears a representation of a horse; when the shaman drums, he is believed to go into the sky on his horse. Among the Buryat, too, the drum made with a horses hide represents that animal. According to O. Mänchen-Helfen, the Soyot shaman's drum is regarded as a horse and is called *khamu-at*, literally 'shaman-horse'. Among certain Mongol tribes the shamanic drum is called the 'black stag'. Where the skin is from a roebuck, the drum is 'the shaman's roebuck' (Karagas, Soyot). Yakut legends tell in detail of the shaman flying through the seven skies with his drum. 'I am travelling with a wild roebuck!' the Karagas and Soyot shamans sing. And the stick with which the drum is beaten is called 'whip' among the Altaians.[60]

With this borne in mind, it is possible that our sources may simply take the drum as a given, without mentioning it. Any journey undertaken to the spirit world by means of horses or similar transport (for example, boats) may be veiled references to a shamanic drum:

> All these beliefs, images, and symbols in relation to the 'flight', the 'riding', or the 'speed' of shamans are figurative expressions for ecstasy, that is, for mystical journeys undertaken by superhuman means and in regions inaccessible to mankind.[61]

We can see this mode of expression illustrated in the following verses from the Tuvan shamans of Siberia (the same peoples who are masters of overtone harmonics, another mode of entering shamanic trance, discussed in greater detail in section two: *Gaining Possession of a Sacrality*).

> Oh! my many-coloured drum
> Ye who standeth in the forward corner!
> Oh! My merry and painted drum,
> Ye who standeth here!
> Let thy shoulder and neck be strong.
>
> Hark, oh hark my horse – ye female maral deer!
> Hark, oh hark my horse – ye bear!
> Hark, oh hark ye [bear]!
>
> Oh, painted drum who standeth in the forward corner!
> My mounts – me and female maral deer.
> Be silent sonorous drum,
> Skin covered drum,
> Fulfil my wishes.
>
> Like flitting clouds, carry me
> Through the lands of dusk
> And below the leaden sky,
> Sweep along like wind
> Over the mountain peaks![62]

Viewing such materials in this way brings into focus a number of other factors arising from the sources. For example, Mogh

Roith's name appears to imply that the 'wheel' was given mystical significance. *Mogh Roith* translates to 'servant of the wheel' – a fitting title for a shaman if the 'wheel' is taken to mean 'drum'. Similarly, Medh and Aillil's druid MacRoth translates to 'son of the wheel'. *Roth* is specifically translated as the 'wheel of a cart' (such as that represented on the Gundestrup cauldron earlier and on other similar images in early Celtic art). Such a title would make little sense outside of a shamanic context. Interestingly, the modern Scots Gaelic word for drum (*druma*) is derived from a word relating to the cart (*drumach* – the 'ridge-band of a cart horse').[63]

In addition to the above, some words used to describe druid's equipment have not been satisfactorily translated. One of these may relate to the shamanic drum. Mogh Roith and his daughter Tlachtga both use the *roth rámach* as a component of their gear in the spirit flight. *Ramach* can mean 'branch', as in the phrase *fri fidrad fonnrám* ('a wood of delicious boughs'[64]); and *roth* means wheel. This pairing may suggest beater and drum like the Altaian example of 'horse' and 'whip' above.[65]

There are a number of references in early Irish sources which appear to support his link between the wheel and the drum. One comes from *Imacallam in Da Thuarad*. Nede asks Fechertne by what path he came. In the course of his answer, he replies:

> *... for creitt cen fonnad, for fonnad cen chul* [66]
> ...on a chariot without a wheelrim, on wheelrim without a chariot.[67]

This may be suggestive of a shamanic spirit journey.

Aldhouse-Green appears to support the hypothesis of early development in relation to the Celtic drum. In Balkåkra, Sweden, a bronze item popularly labelled a 'sun-drum' has been found. It consists of a cylindrical object, roughly sixteen inches in diameter, supporting a flat disc decorated with circular designs and mounted on ten miniature spoked 'wheels'. Aldhouse-Green surmises:

Its size and appearance suggests that it may have been utilised as some kind of drum or table, perhaps used in a similar manner to a shaman's drum, both as a percussive device and as a means of plotting the future, maybe in conjunction with rods, counters or other items that could be cast 'at random' on its surface.[68]

In addition to this example, we find depictions of 'ecstatic frenzy' on some Breton coins dating from the Iron Age.[69] Interestingly for this study, such images usually depict individuals carrying spoked, wheel-like instruments.

The association of such 'wheel' images with the shaman's drum becomes less far-fetched when held up against more traditionally shamanic depictions of this instrument. Examples of Siberian rock art appear to show almost identical images of wheels in an ecstatic context. Devlet suggests that these images represent the spoked drum of the Siberian shaman:

As is well known, the different Siberian peoples frequently used drums as an essential component of their ritual activities. These drums varied in their form, and alongside those of predominantly circular shape in certain regions one may also find drums with an ovoid construction.[70]

Of the wheel symbol, Devlet goes on to add that 'this pattern is repeated in the drums shown in the rock art, on engraved plaques, and depicted on various other ritual items … it [the drum] served as a shaman's mode of transportation for visits to other spheres of the universe'.[71]

The drum is not the only means of obtaining percussive sounds, however. The CD produced by the Kilmartin House Museum, *The Kilmartin Sessions: The Sounds of Ancient Scotland*, attempts to recreate 'sounds that would have been familiar to our forebears thousands of years ago'.[72] Track number four of this CD demonstrates the percussive quality of 'ringing rocks' – stones which have an inherent natural resonance when struck by another stone. The Tiree Ringing Rock and the Druid Rock on Iona are two examples of this which have an abundance of local folklore attached to them. They are recorded demonstrating variation in pitch depending upon where they are struck.

Another example is the lithophone, or stone xylophone. Track five of *The Kilmartin Sessions* recreates the sound of a four note lithophone found by Colonel Fane Gladwin on a beach near Loch Fyne. This is an instrument which 'could have been played upon at any time since the coming of man. All it requires is to strike or stroke the stones with a piece of hard wood'.[73]

In addition to these, Aldhouse-Green suggests that the rattle found among a religious hoard from Felmingham Hall in Norfolk and dating from the Romano-British period may also have been used to shamanic effect.[74] Other examples of sound as a means of entering shamanic trance will be discussed in the second section.

With the weight of this evidence it is impossible to discount the theory that the early Celts possessed drums. I agree with Trevarthen's note that the drum is a very primitive instrument possessed by most cultures across the globe (whether operating within a shamanic mode of perception or not), and it would be surprising if early Celtic tribes did not possess this basic instrument.

oOo

It would be impossible to go into detail on all the other forms of shamanic equipment mentioned in the early Irish source material. Others include Fionn's crane bag, the four treasures of the *Tuatha Dé Dánnan*, magical cauldrons and all the paraphernalia associated with drinking. Each of the above appear to relate to spiritual power.[75]

Pliny said that the druids 'hold nothing more sacred than the mistletoe' and the tree upon which it grows – especially if this

33

was an oak. 'Hailing the moon in a native word that means "healing all things" they prepare a ritual sacrifice.' This consisted of two white bulls, and was made after a priest had cut the mistletoe with a golden sickle.[76] The fact that the priest's robes and implement, the bulls and the mistletoe all share a similar colour-scheme may indicate a totemic identification of priest, sacred plant, and bulls. The 'golden sickle', then, may be a magical implement only used by shamans to ritually significant effect.

Ritual knives in shamanism appear to be most commonly found in the east. Lolo shamanism, which appears to have been heavily influenced by Chinese magic, utilises a number of ritual knives in a ritual known as the 'ladder of knives'. This ritual is also found in China, and the Lolo shaman's name for their ritual knife (as well as their words for 'drum' and 'spirits') comes from Chinese.[77]

However, perhaps the most obvious piece of shamanic equipment in the vernacular sources is the *craebh ciúil*, or 'musical branch'. This was a stick which usually had three bells on it and was carried by the *filidh*, who used it to signal the start of meetings, to bring peace to assemblies, and to play the music of *súantraige*. The branch nourishes and produces harmonious sounds.[78]

The *craebh ciúil* was said to be able to bring peace to even the most agitated mob. In *Mesca Ulaid* the *filidh* Sencha, Conchobar's chief advisor, was the only one who was able to restore order by using his *craebh ciúil*.[79] In *Fled Bricrend* he again shakes his 'peace-keeping branch' to stop a potential battle.[80] A *craebh ciúil* is given to king Cormac by a figure who is apparently his spirit teacher. Finally, at the end of *Serglige Con Culainn*, Mannanan Mac Lir shakes his musical branch between Cú Chulainn and Fand 'so that they might never meet together again throughout eternity'.[81]

The music of *súantraige* that the branch plays appears to be a light, trance inducing state. It is able to pacify – the Old Irish word *súan* means 'sleep'. The quality of this sleep appears to be transformative, as the name 'peace-keeping branch' appears to suggest.

There are numerous references to similar instruments used in shamanistic contexts in other cultures. In the initiation ceremony of the Carib shaman, it is normal for up to six youths to be initiated at the same time. During this process, 'each of them makes his own bells and a "magical staff" six feet long'.[82] Among the equipment of the Siberian shaman can be found 'magical sticks, bells, and very many kinds of drums'.[83]

A close comparison of *craebh ciúil* can be found in the bough Aeneas carries into the Underworld in Vergil's *Aeneid*. Charon is taken by surprise at the sight of the bough, 'rarely seen in Hades'. Hull takes this to mean that 'it was only those who entered the realms of the dead in life who presented the branch to Proserpine'.[84] If this is the case, we have a clear candidate for a shamanic piece of equipment.

With these interpretations, we are able to look on the Old Irish material in a new light – no longer do we see as if through a glass darkly, but with more focus and understanding of how a now chronologically removed culture may have thought and acted. Seeing our sources with a shamanistic eye, I would argue, is the only way to gain such an understanding of these texts.

Stone on top of stone, and the wall goes up...

There are a great many 'transitional objects' to be found in the source literature that it would be impossible to go into detail with all of them. However, I believe that the above represents a trend which corresponds to the classical equipment of the shaman, facilitating a shamanistic relationship between costume, instrument and practitioner.

35

We see this relationship repeatedly in the literary sources, and not just in Old Irish traditions. The tale of Taliesin, for example, where Cerridwen and Taliesin continually change shape during the chase, deals with this relationship in detail.[85] To find the most famous example, though, we must again turn to the Old Irish tradition, and the words of Amergin White-Knee recorded in the *Lebor Gabála:*

Am gáeth i mmuir,	I am wind on sea,
Am tonn trethain,	I am ocean wave,
Am fúaimm mara,	I am the roar of the sea,
Am tarb secht ndrenn,	I am a bull of seven fights,
Am séig i n-aill,	I am vulture on a cliff,
Am dér gréne,	I am a teardrop of the sun,
Am caín lubae,	I am the most beautiful of flowers,
Am torc ar gáil,	I am a boar of boldness,
Am hé i llind,	I am a salmon in water,
Am loch i mmaig,	I am a lake in the plain,
Am brí dánae,	I am a word of song,
Am gae i fodb feras fechtu.	I am the point of a weapon.
Am dé delbas do chin codnu.[86]	I am a God who makes fire in the head.[87]

Given our knowledge of shamanic costuming, we are now in a position to pose a new interpretation on these mystical lines of poetry. The association of the self with animal spirits through costuming and the spirit flight could lead to the experience of seeing into all things and experiencing them as part of the self. In Amergin's song, the self is no longer merely associated with animal forms, but also with the elements of nature and with more abstract concepts. This unites the shaman with the universal order around them, increasing their power and standing among their community. The shaman, in this mode, acts as a representative for the cosmic order, physically incarnate among their people.

The costume adorning the shaman can take many forms, but almost always has animal associations (even if it is not made

36

from the skin of said animal). This is consistent with what we know of shamanistic cultures in general, and their animistic world-view. The Celtic tradition provides us with numerous parallels to these examples.

The importance of the drum in shamanic cultures has already been elucidated. As the vehicle for ecstatic journeying, a core tenet of shamanism, its evolution seems to be virtually universal throughout the shamanistic world. We have a number of possible references in source material which draw striking resemblances to classically shamanic cultures, together with some iconographic and archaeological evidence to support the claim that the druids may have utilised this most basic of instruments in their rituals. The 'spoked' appearance of the potential drum shown on the Gundestrup cauldron could parallel the picture opposite of a Mongolian shaman carrying a similar 'spoked drum' in the same posture. Perhaps one points towards the other.

Due to the perishable nature of the material discussed, it is impossible to gain much of an understanding of primal Celtic drums. What we can theorise can only be suggested through

Mongolian Shaman circa 1905

implications in surviving texts and iconography, which are necessarily fallible, subjective sources. What I have presented is one possible interpretation for the material; one which I believe to be consistent with the shamanic nature of Celtic traditional practice. These conclusions are shared by a number of scholars, who believe the drum to have a more ancient pedigree in Ireland. O'Dwyer goes as far as to suggest that the *bodhrán* – still in use in modern Celtic folk music – dates from around 4,000 – 6,000 BCE.

> There is a school of opinion that the bodhrán is in fact a very recent addition to the Irish musical instrument repertoire. This seems unlikely when considering the commonality of frame drums throughout the prehistoric world... If the origins of the bodhrán date back to the Stone Age, we are indeed fortunate to have such a vibrant living connection with our early ancestors.[88]

The use of magical costuming and instruments such as the drum are not merely confined to the shamanic séance however. Many shamans drum and sing for their own pleasure, enhancing their interaction with spirit. The implications of this remain the same: ascension to spirit in order to visit the otherworld. This, according to Eliade, eventually leads to the costuming and instruments gaining an 'autonomy' of their own, separate from the practitioner.

> This 'autonomy' to which instruments of magico-religious music finally attain has led to the constitution of a magic that, if not yet 'profane', is certainly freer and more vivid than a purely religious music. The same phenomenon is observable in connection with the shamanic songs that narrate ecstatic journeys to the sky and dangerous descents to the underworld.[89]

In his definitive work, *Shamanism: Archaic Techniques of Ecstasy*, Eliade attempts to provide an evolutionary map of religious experience. Shamanism and animism feature early on in religious development, but this must not be confused with a primitive or naïve world-view. Eliade concludes that shamanism eventually evolves out of itself:

> After a time adventures of this kind [spirit journeys] pass into the folklore of the respective peoples and enrich popular oral literature with new themes and characters.[90]

This is an evolution which can be clearly seen in later Celtic folklore and folk traditions, permitting a truer understanding of how primal Celtic shamanism never completely died out. Evidence for shamanistic practice and ritual can be found in abundance in later Gaelic oral traditions and folk memory. Before we can deal with this, however, we must now turn our attention to the symptoms of primal Celtic shamanism as indicated through ritual and spiritual practice.

PART TWO

GAINING POSSESSION OF A SACRALITY

He had drunk, and now he softly sang. Gradually, faint lines and forms began to appear in the darkness, and the shrill music of the *tsentsak*, the spirit helpers, arose around him. The power of the drink fed them. He called, and they came. First, *pangi*, the anaconda, coiled about his head, transmuted into a crown of gold. Then *wampang*, the giant butterfly, hovered above his shoulder and sang to him with its wings. Snakes, spiders, birds, and bats danced in the air above him. On his arms appeared a thousand eyes as his demon helpers emerged to search the night for enemies.

Michael Harner - 'The Sound of Rushing Water'

Be you a smooth way before me…

> This god's a prophet, too, for those rituals –
> the Bacchic celebrations and the madness –
> unleash considerable prophetic power.
> When the god enters the body fully,
> he makes those possessed by frenzy prophets.
> They speak of what's to happen in the future.
>
> Euripides, *The Bacchae*

F undamental to the shamanic condition is the ability to travel at will between the physical realm and the realm of the spirits. Seeing the spirits, either as manifest in physical form, or by travelling to spiritual reality, is a certain sign that the shaman has – in some way – gained what Eliade describes as a 'spiritual condition': one where boundaries between the material and the spiritual become indistinct. It is a sign that the shaman has, by voluntary and deliberate means, transcended the 'profane' condition of humanity to the 'sacred' condition of spirit.

Among the Mentaweians, the spirit vision has the effect of bestowing special abilities, or *kerei*, upon the shaman. Andaman shamans withdraw into the solitude of the jungle to obtain their visions, believing that those who have received communications solely through dreams merely obtain inferior spiritual powers. Similarly, among the Menangkabau of Sumatra, the *dukun* complete their shamanic training in the solitude of the mountains. They learn to become invisible, and at night, see the spirits of the dead, '…they *become* spirits … they *are* dead'.[1] This removal from civilisation and participation in death is reminiscent of the way that Mis withdraws from civilisation in the tale *Aithed Muirne re Dubh Ruis*, seen in the previous section. In shamanic cultures, this personal interaction with the sacred is made possible by the ability to enter a trance state.

According to Eliade, trance is the 'syndrome of gaining possession of a sacrality',[2] a state of being where the self dissolves into the sacred, which encompasses all sensory functions. In trance, the shaman often experiences an ecstasy of spirit, an unbridled joy which finds few comparisons. One account by an Inuit shaman describes his experience of trance thus:

> ...I felt a great, inexplicable joy, a joy so powerful I could not restrain it, but had to break into song, a mighty song, with only room for one word: joy, joy! And I had to use the full strength of my voice. And then in the midst of such a fit of mysterious and overwhelming delight I became a shaman ... I could see and hear in a totally different way.[3]

Freed from physical sensation, the shaman is able to receive clearly the energy of the spirits. This experience of the self freed from psychological limitations is what many mystics in various cultures have deemed to be the 'true self'.

We can define trance, then, as a technique which not only brings the practitioner into contact with the spirits, but also with the most free and sacred parts of their essential self. Given this precept, it is no wonder that shamanic practice has survived in Celtic and other regions.

A psychological study of Yogic practice reveals that the main aim of meditation (a light trance state) is to escape the suffering and the ordinariness of real life. The removal of emotional distress appears, then, to be the focus behind this practice; thus a differentiation is made between the primary and secondary selves: that which is active in physical reality; and that which is active in spiritual reality.[4] In this way, trance can be seen to have transformative and healing qualities; an altered state of consciousness which transcends emotional stresses.

From a scientific perspective, trance is seen mainly as a physical phenomenon – an anaesthetised state which stimulates areas of the brain more commonly associated with dreaming. With this in mind, we are able to gain a more rounded understanding of what this experience is. Trance combines the relaxative qualities of a good night's sleep with the adrenal 'high' of strenuous exercise. Working between these polarities, we find the shaman.

In some cultures, trance is seen to be a kind of death. When the shaman enters an ecstatic state, he is considered to belong to the spirit world, no longer a part of material reality. When the shaman returns, he is thought to have transcended death. We can see this through traditional initiation ceremonies in a number of cultures. Among the Araucanians, a neophyte will fall 'as if dead' and upon recovery will declare themselves a *machi* (shaman).[5] The 'ghost ceremony' of the Pomo involves the torture, death, and subsequent resurrection of the neophytes. Similar rituals are found among the Yuki, the Huchnom and the Coast Miwok.[6]

We can see clearly from the above that the experience of trance is often synonymous with the experience of death. When the shaman comes out of trance, he is said to have been resurrected by the spirits, hence the shaman's traditional role as 'walker between the worlds'. Having experienced death and returned to life, the shaman is able to enter the spirit world at will. In this way, they are seen as a physical incarnation of the natural order – through death and resurrection the shaman represents and reinforces the natural cycle from life to death back to life.

Into the Mist

Did the druids in primal Celtic society practice ecstatic trance? Contemporary classical observers appear to suggest that they did. Pomponius Mela, writing during the reign of Claudius, the fourth emperor of the Roman Empire, noted:

These [druids] profess to know the size and shape of the world, the movements of the heavens and of the stars, and the will of the gods. They teach many things to the nobles of Gaul in a course of instruction lasting as long as twenty years, meeting in secret either in a cave or in secluded dales.[7]

The secrecy element of druidic teachings is echoed in the later spiritual practices of the Gaels as recorded by Alexander Carmichael in his *Carmina Gadelica.* Carmichael records that reciters 'generally retire to a closet, an outhouse, to the lee of a knoll, or to the shelter of a dell, that they may not be seen nor heard'.[8]

This stress on privacy and secrecy lends a mystic air to Celtic religious practice, one which is again shored up by contemporaneous observations. Diogenes Laertius, writing in the third century ACE, compared the druids to the Persian magi and the Indian 'gymnosophists'. He says that 'the gymnosophists and the druids make their pronouncements by means of riddles and dark sayings',[9] recalling the ecstatic oracular function of the *Pythia* at Delphi. The modern Gaelic word for oracle is *guth-aite*, or 'place of voice', as it was believed that the spirits or gods spoke directly through the human vessel. In the case of the *Pythia*, the voice of Apollo could not be expressed by the human tongue, resulting in an ecstatic 'fit' possibly brought on by the use of psychotropic substances.

'Channelling' the spirits is a common feature of the shamanic séance. Usually, this possession is involuntary, as in the case of *lwa* possession in Vodou rituals. Eliade points out that when someone is possessed by a spirit 'he speaks in a strange voice and prophesies'.[10] In New Guinea, possession by an ancestral spirit is employed voluntary in order to seek their advice.

When someone is ill, or it is wished to discover something unknown, a member of the family takes the image of the dead relative whose counsel is to be asked, sets it on his knees or his shoulder, and lets himself be possessed by the dead person's soul.[11]

Perhaps this is the experience Laertius was trying to relate, although he lacked the necessary cultural precedents with which to frame his comments.

o0o

If the ancient Celts were to have entered a state of trance, we would expect to find a language with which to frame this state of consciousness. We have already seen how *geltacht* may indicate a similar level of consciousness, although with more reference to madness than death. The Old Irish word *serglige*, however, may shed further light on the argument.

In the 'Wasting Sickness of Cú Chulainn', the eponymous protagonist is beaten by the spirits into a year long catatonic state. He lies for this time, as if dead, whilst his spirit is engaged in the otherworld, increasing his spiritual powers. This experience is not too far removed from the shamanic death described earlier. *Serglige* is translated as 'wasting sickness', as the sufferer is unable to eat or drink or move whilst inflicted by it. The resulting coma causes them to appear dead to the outsider – a more exact parallel with shamanic initiation would be hard to find.

Interestingly, however, there is such a parallel in the modern Scots Gaelic language. As we shall see in the third section, many shamanic functions and philosophies have been preserved in the semantics of the Gaelic language; giving rise to a number of perceived linguistic peculiarities. One of these is how the trance state is expressed: *neul a' bhàis*, literally 'in the mist of death'.[12] Interestingly Ross notes that the word *bàs*, or 'death', is usually reserved for animals: 'Of a human being people say

47

chahchail e, 'he changed', or *shiubhail e*, 'he travelled'.[13] It appears that the Gaels both acknowledged the trance state in their language, and also adopted a shamanic mode of expression to convey it.

Interestingly, the word *neul* has many mystical connotations. Originally, the art of *neuladaireachd* meant 'cloud-gazing' – a form of divination which the classical authors attribute to the druids. Nowadays in modern Gaelic this term has kept its divinatory connotations and means 'astrology'.

The word *neul* is derived from the Old Irish word *nél* (Welsh *niwl*), whose primary meaning is 'mist'. Perhaps this derivation reveals a cultural association between mist and trance, the former descriptive of the type of 'death' invoked by the latter. Used as an adjective, *neulach* can mean both 'cloudy' and 'sickly', or 'pale', again reminiscent of the sickness associated with initiatory ordeals in shamanic cultures, and the *serglige* of Cú Chulainn.

In making this association, those who enter a trance state in Gaelic are seen to be participating in death. We can see a possible reference to this in the *imbas forosnai* ecstatic ritual in Irish traditions. The etymology of the term *imbas* (often translated as 'inspired' or 'poetic knowledge') is commonly given as 'in the hands' *im* (in) + *bas* (hands). It is also possible, though, that *bás* may have been intended instead of *bas*. If this is true, then a more correct translation would be 'in death' – supporting the shamanic mode of perception surviving in the modern Scots Gaelic language. The details of the ecstatic ritual *imbas forosnai* will be discussed in detail later in this section.

We can accept from this linguistic evidence, then, that both Old Irish and modern Scots Gaelic traditions both accept the use of trance within their respective culturally defined vocabularies. We must now look at how this was achieved.

oOo

Trance can be seen primarily as a physical phenomenon, effecting bodily functions and brain wave patterns to invoke an anaesthetised state. This being the case, perhaps it is most appropriate that we begin our analysis of trance in primal Celtic traditions with physical indicators.

Harner mentions psychotropic drugs as one of the most common modes of entering trance in shamanic cultures. He makes a case study of the Jívaro entheogen *ayahuasca* ('the little death'), describing its effects on his own body when convinced to partake of it. The resulting trance leads him into a number of shamanic worlds and experiences. In his account, he is laid out in a darkened room and left alone, again in imitation of, or participation in, death.

> As I stared upward into the darkness, faint lines of light appeared. They grew sharper, more intricate, and burst into brilliant colours. Sound came from far away, a sound like a waterfall, which grew stronger and stronger until it filled my ears.[14]

Many other cultures employ entheogens to achieve a trance state. Siberian shamans, for example, class psychotropics along with the drum and zither as the 'great' material means by which 'the Ungarian magician attempts to communicate with the spirits'.[15]

Could the Celts have used entheogens to stimulate trance? They certainly came into contact with cultures who did. The Scythians, for example, were aware of the consciousness altering properties of cannabis. Herodotus reported that the Scythians threw cannabis seeds on hot stones and inhaled the resulting smoke, which caused them to fall about and roar with delight afterwards.[16]

Perhaps a ritual use of entheogens can be found in Celtic culture in the form of the mistletoe cutting ceremony. As highlighted in the previous section for its totemic associations,

49

the mistletoe cutting ceremony was considered to be one of the most sacred rites performed by the druids. According to Pliny, the cutting was performed by a white-robed druid using a golden or bronze sickle on the sixth day of the moon. 'They chose this day because, although the moon has not yet reached half-size, it already has considerable influence.'[17] Afterwards, a sacrifice was made.

Pliny said that the druids 'hold nothing more sacred than the mistletoe' and the tree upon which it grows. The reason for the plant's importance is not recorded, however, leaving the ethnobiologist to guess at its significance. The most obvious explanation would be to suggest that the berries of the plant were consumed in a ritualistic manner. Cooper and Johnson's *Poisonous Plants in Britain and their Effects on Animals and Man* describes the symptoms induced by ingesting mistletoe berries as 'including pale lips, inflammation of the eyes, dilated pupils, slow pulse, laboured breathing, hallucinations and coma'.[18] All these symptoms are conducive with trance as given above. They go on to add that 'severity of the symptoms varies with the number of berries eaten',[19] suggesting that the level of trance invoked could be controlled under the correct guidance.

Interestingly, Lindow Man (a 'bog body' discovered in Lindow Moss, Cheshire, in 1984) had consumed a small quantity of mistletoe pollen before he died. As traces were found in his digestive tract, it is very likely that these were eaten more or less immediately prior to death, suggesting a ritualistic use related to human sacrifice and death.[20]

Each of these factors strongly indicate that mistletoe, as the most sacred of plants, was used in order to facilitate the spirit flight among the druids. As specialists in the sacred, the druids would be able to take advantage of this technique to come into a closer, more personal and interactive union with the Sacred.

o0o

Entheogens were not the only methods employed by shamans to reach this state, however. Harner describes 'chant' and 'drumming' to be two of the most common methods as well as psychotropic drugs. We have already discussed the probability of percussive sound for invocation of trance in the first section, so we will now turn our attention to the power of the voice.

Fionn and his war band were said to have been able to perform a chant known as *dordfhiansa* – a sound so powerful it was said be able to scatter an entire army when sung.[21] The meaning of this word is difficult to pin down, although it is probable that the *dord* element relates to *dordán*, *sordán* and other words for 'droning, humming' etc. In performing this chant, the Fianna were said to have pursed lips – a technique which calls to mind Tuvan overtone chanting.

Overtones, a phenomenon occurring naturally when any sound is created, refer to the partial tones which carry over the top of the fundamental base note. They are higher in frequency and are perceived in a natural harmonic order. From ancient times, the Tuva, living north of Mongolia, have practiced traditional throat music and overtone harmonics. De Ruiter describes the process:

> Overtone singing – also called *guttural*, *throat* or *biphonal* singing – originates when one singer simultaneously generates a fundamental and one or several overtones. The melody is conveyed by overtones in a high register, while a drone (the same note played or sung continuously) serves as the fundamental. In some styles of overtone singing the performer adds tone coloration to the fundamental, creating a triple-voice effect. It is said that overtones are imitations of sounds in nature, like the wind in high mountains or the water in fast-flowing rivers.[22]

Research into the physical effects of overtone harmonic singing is still in its infancy, although some early pointers appear to suggest effects on brain-wave patterns. The effect of a large group of warriors all performing overtone chanting would have a very powerful psychological effect on any person witness to it, hence the effects described by the *dordfhiansa*.

There is another possible reference to overtone harmonic singing in primal Celtic culture in the work of the much derided Iolo Morgannwg. Morgannwg's evidence was said to be copied directly from an ancient source manuscript detailing the rituals and practices of the ancient druids of Britain. This was later discredited when a number of draft copies were found after Morgannwg's death. Nevertheless, these sources do provide an interesting correspondence with overtone harmonics, and are included here *cum grano salis.*

The *Barddas* states that the creation reaction began when God spoke the *awen*. This sound radiated out throughout the universe in the form of three bars of light. Each bar had a corresponding sound, given in the *Barddas* as O-I-V. In respect of this creation myth, Morgannwg states that Welsh bards sang the three notes *simultaneously* in imitation of God. *Barddas* states that whilst the O-I-V could be sung, 'they could not be pronounced'.[23] This gives a strong indication that these three sounds were produced using overtone harmonics – which can be sung simultaneously, but cannot be pronounced when spoken. Trevarthen notes that one of the simplest ways to begin overtone chanting is to go from an O, to an I, concluding in a bilabial V or U sound.[24]

With this reported practice, we find another interesting synchronicity with the 'bars of light' in the Tuvan tradition. One harmonic overtone group, called *Huun-Huur-Tu*, takes its name from the 'rays of light that come down through clouds'. They chose this name because the 'light rays on the steppe remind us of the separate lines of sound in throat singing, except that in throat singing you're working not with light rays but with sound rays'.[25]

The descendant of this practice is hinted at in the later hagiographies of Celtic saints. Both St. Brendan and St. Columba were reputed to have had considerable vocal powers, suggestive of overtone harmonic singing. St. Columba's biographer, Adomnan, reports that he occasionally sang 'spiritual chants of a kind never heard before'. Buckley notes that he was also famous for singing psalms with a voice like thunder, or a melodious lion. He is said to have terrified Brude, the Pictish king, by singing the forty-fourth psalm in a voice that 'rose in the air like a terrible thunderstorm'.[26]

This kind of harmonic is also evident in early Celtic musical instruments. Purser noted that if the Carnyx (a Celtic boar-like war trumpet) was blown in the same way as the Aboriginal didgeridoo, it would produce the same kind of sound. Track twenty-three of Kilmartin House Museum's *The Kilmartin Sessions* demonstrates how this may have sounded. A later Celtic war instrument, the bagpipe, also demonstrates an overtone sound. Perhaps when the practice of vocal overtoning became less specialist, it was incorporated into religious and military instrumentation.

We find comparable instruments in other classically shamanic cultures as well. Other than the didgeridoo, we find the mouth harp and singing bowl – both from the Himalayas. In the case of the latter, the pitch of the over- and under-tones can be varied with the size, shape and thickness of the bowl itself. Traditionally, Tibetan singing bowls are thick and deep, making a sound which is 'pure, long-lasting and lush'.[27] The mouth harp, on the other hand, is a simple piece of metal, held against the lips, and vibrated using the fingers. The overtones produced and varied according to the shape of the mouth and throat, and through variance in breathing techniques.

The practice of singing in an overtone harmonic is not restricted to the Tuvans and Celts, however: throat singing resonates throughout the Mongolian region. The ancient

Chinese, Hindus and Greeks (such as Pythagoras) all discovered harmonics.[28] Harmonic resonances such as those sung by the Tuvans are described by de Ruiter as 'primal' as the fundamental keynote, or drone (*dordan*), is likened to the primordial creation myth surrounding many cultures: '*In the beginning there was Sound*'.[29]

The transformative effects of overtone harmonics are only beginning to be realised. Preliminary research has highlighted effects on brain-wave patterns, with possible consciousness altering qualities.

> Our consciousness determines the vibration of our brain waves. Our brain radiates various wavelengths, depending on the state we are in. When we are very excited, or working hard, the *beta waves* (12 Hz and higher up) are dominant; when more relaxed we are producing *alpha waves* (8-12 Hz), when very relaxed or in meditation, the brainwaves are predominantly *theta* (4-8 Hz), and when in very deep meditation, or sleeping, we produce mostly *delta* (4 Hz and lower). Various combinations of these states are possible throughout our days and nights. Music can certainly influence our brain states, and so can overtones. Many listeners at overtone concerts report a complete change of consciousness, lasting from half an hour to several days...[30]

Its use in inducing shamanic trance, then, becomes apparent – resting overtone chanting firmly within our bounds of research. Unfortunately, the consciousness altering effects of such techniques requires much further study as their full efficacy remains largely undiscovered.

o0o

No matter how the trance state was achieved in Celtic culture, either through percussive sound, entheogens or chant; we must acknowledge that the means and abilities were there for Celts and druids alike to take advantage of. A further scrutiny of primal Celtic religious practice reveals how such techniques were employed to shamanic effect. It is with these rituals and practices in mind that we now turn our focus toward ideas of poetic inspiration in primal Celtic tradition.

Exstasis in Sacred Practice

A boriginal beliefs portray the primordial spirit realm as the 'Dreaming' – the source of creation and the home of the spirits. A well trained shaman may pass into the Dreaming and commune with the spirits of tribal ancestors and totemic animals in furtherance of their spiritual aims. Eliade records how potential shamans are laid out, as if dead, in order to experience the Dreaming, the spirit world. They may be left for several nights, without sustenance.[31]

The purpose of entering into the Dreaming, according to most aboriginal tribes, is generally prophetic. Such mantic practices find their relatives in Celtic religious practice, noted by Cormac in his famous 10th Century *Glossary* in the form of *imbas forosnai* , *dichetal do chennaib*, and *tenm laida.* Of these three, *imbas forosnai* has been subject of the most research, and as a result is the one which we know most about.

The shamanic significance of *imbas*' obscured etymology has already been highlighted. The passage in Cormac's *Glossary* explaining the practice is similarly obscure, almost rendering it untranslatable. For the purposes of this analysis I have used both Stokes's and Meyer's translations – the former for a broad picture, and the latter to flesh out some language difficulties inherent in the text.

According to Stokes' translation, Cormac's *Glossary* reports:

> *Imbas forosna*, 'Manifestation that enlightens': (it) discovers what thing soever the poet likes and which he desires to reveal. Thus then is that done. The poet chews

a piece of the red flesh of a pig, or a dog, or a cat, and puts it then on a flagstone behind the door-valve, and chants an incantation over it, and offers it to idol gods, and calls them to him, and leaves them not on the morrow, and then chants over his two palms, and calls again idol gods to him, that his sleep may not be disturbed. Then he puts his two palms on his two cheeks and sleeps. And men are watching him that he may not turn over and that no one may disturb him. And then is revealed to him that for which he was (engaged) till the end of a *nomad* (three days and nights), or two or three for the long or the short (time?) that he may judge himself (to be) at the offering. And therefore it is called *Imm-bas*, to wit, a palm (*bas*) on this side and a palm on that around his head. Patrick banished that and the tenm laida 'illumination of song' and declared that no one who shall do that shall belong to heaven or earth, for it is a denial of baptism.

Dichetal do chennaib, extempore incantation, however, that was left, in right of art, for it is science that causes it, and no offering to devils is necessary, but a declaration from the ends of his bones at once.[32]

The importance of this practice is testified by a number of sources. In a gloss to a passage on the seven poetical grades contained in the *Uraicecht Becc* we are told that there are three things required of an *ollamh*-poet: 'teinm laegda', 'imus forosnad' and 'dichetal do chennaib'.[33] The Nemed-Judgements also say: 'three things which dignify the dignities of a poet, 'tenm laegda', 'imus forosnad', 'dichetal do chennaib'.[34]

These practices appear to be the preserve of the *filidh* – the shamanic poets. In an article for the *Scottish Gaelic Studies* journal, Chadwick described the process of *imbas forosnai* as both 'mantic sleep' and 'revelation', likening it to a number of shamanic trance practices.[35] The 'sleep' certainly appears to have a prophetic intention. A similar technique can be found in Polynesian shamanism.[36] Among the Naidu 'one becomes a shaman by dreaming of spirits'.[37] The image of the North American shaman seeking a vision quest is also invoked.

In almost all examples of this kind, a ritual darkness is observed. Darkness is very important for trance as it blocks out any visual stimulus which could bring the consciousness back into material reality. This could be the intention behind placing the palms over the eyes in *imbas forosnai*.

Chewing animal flesh in preparation for 'mantic sleep' is also significant, and points towards a possible totemic relationship. The three meats mentioned are pig, dog and cat. We already know the totemic significance of the dog inherent in the name Cú Chulainn ('the dog of Culainn'). In this case, however, eating dog flesh is *geis* (taboo) for the warrior, with terrible consequences if broken.

Cat would have been an unusual meat to the ancient Celts. Cat burials have been found both at Danebury and Gussage All Saints[38] and the archaeological record preserves an image of a wild cat at the Camonica Valley,[39] all dating from the Celtic period. Associations with Celtic tribes are also suggested in modern Gaelic place names. Caithness, in northern Scotland, for example, takes its name from the Gaelic for cat; and early Roman maps call Shetland 'Isle of Cats' and Orkney 'Isle of Dogs'.

Evidence for the totemic representation of pigs and boars is numerous. The Carnyx gives one good example; as do the animal helmeted warriors on the side of the Gundestrup cauldron depicted in the first section. All of this together may lead one to conclude that the specification of meats for *imbas forosnai* may represent such a totemic relationship.

Chewing as a monotonous task is a good way to focus the attention, which could be another side-effect of this practice. Pig, dog and cat flesh are all quite tough, taking some amount of chewing! If a totemic relationship is in evidence with these animals, chewing their flesh may also represent an attempt to adopt the spiritual powers of the animal in furtherance of shamanic goals.

Chewing is also a significant motif in other Old Irish sagas concerning enlightenment and revelation. It has been mentioned in the *Macgnimartha Find* that Fionn learned *imbas forosnai*, *tenm laida* and *dichetal do chennaib* as part of his training in poetry. The *Senchas Mór* contains a tale known as 'Fionn and the Man in the Tree' which has Fionn trap his finger in the door of a *Sid* mound. Fionn then 'puts his thumb into his mouth. When he takes it out again, his *imbas* illuminates him and he chants an incantation'.[40] In order to reaccess this inspired knowledge, he must chew his thumb 'from the skin to the bone, from the bone to the marrow, and from the marrow to the inner marrow'.[41]

In Stokes's translation of the *Glossary*, men surround the practitioner in search of *imbas* in order to ensure they are not disturbed. This is reminiscent of a scene from *Serglige Con Culainn*, and may also have shamanic significance. Cú Chulainn is inflicted by a spiritual 'wasting sickness' which keeps him in a catatonic state for a year. Whilst in this state, his friends and wife attend him. Fergus stands by the side wall; Conall at his head, Lugaid at his pillow and Emer is at his feet.[42]

These two scenes call to mind the image of a young Bushman being called back from the spirit journey.[43] Deep in trance, *ntum* masters surround him, gently blowing on him, cradling his head and calling him back to material reality. One Bushman described the experience: 'They take hold of your head and blow about the sides of your face. This is how you manage to be alive again. Friends, if they don't do that to you, you die.'[44] This ritual is important as it implies community support for the work of the shaman. Meyer's translation of the *Glossary* has it slightly differently however, stating that the spirits themselves stand guard over the body ensuring the seeker is not disturbed in their search for *imbas*.

References to the 'nuts of *imbas*' in the sources also suggest an alternative method for attaining prophetic trance: one which recalls the use of entheogens or psychotropic drugs. These nuts, or hazels, are associated with sacred rivers (the Springs of Shannon and the Boyne as well as elsewhere).[45] In regard to Fionn, *imbas* was originally derived by eating salmon fed on the hazel nuts at the spring at the source of the Boyne. Hazel nuts themselves have no psychotropic effects, even if eaten in large quantities; however many shamanic communities disguise the name of their drugs with metaphor. For example, Vedic Soma (thought to be the mushroom *amanita muscaria*[46]) is called variously *máda* (inebriation) and *mádhu* (honey) amongst other titles.

The shamanic power of *imbas* is summed up by Chadwick in relation to the Fionn tales. She concludes that 'it is clear that *imbas forosnai* gives to Finn the power of supernatural vision, and enables him to see the spirit world'.[47]

Examples of *tenm laida* in the sources are harder to find. A tale found in Cormac's *Glossary* relating to Fionn hua Basicne tells how Fionn identifies the corpse (minus head) of his fool *tre tenm laido* - 'by means of tenm laida'. This motif is found among a number of Old Irish tales, leading some to assume that it was a custom for the identification of dead bodies.[48] This seems a little unlikely, as shown in another tale regarding Fionn.

In *Macgnimartha Find* (dating from the twelfth century, or earlier) Fionn cooks and eats the salmon of wisdom in order to gain *imbas*. We are told that in so doing, Fionn gained knowledge of things previously hidden from him. To re-access this knowledge, Fionn need only put his thumb into his mouth and sing through *tenm laida*.[49] Meyer translates the term as 'illumination through song', linking inspired knowledge with music (a concept widespread in Celtic shamanism, and subject of the last chapter in this section *Finding a Language*).

The final attribute of the *ollamh*-poet is *dichetal do chennaib*, translated by Meyer as 'extempore incantation'.[50] From the Old Irish *dican* ('chanting'), *dichetal do chennaib* is recorded by Cormac to have been permitted to continue under Christian supervision by Saint Patrick, as it did not involve sacrificing to pagan gods. The poem by Amergin quoted in part one is an example of *dichetal do chennaib*, already making strong shamanic associations.

Because the chanting of the *filidh* was believed to be magically potent, this term came to be associated with the English 'incantation' as in the *dicetal in druad* in the *Tripartite Life* of Saint Patrick.[51] The use of chanting in shamanic cultures has already been discussed previously as a common method for invoking trance and gaining enlightenment.

Such ecstatic methods are not confined to Ireland however. Giraldus Cambrensis in his 12th Century ACE *Description of Wales* identifies a class of people called *Awenyddion*, who appear to practice an art closely resembling those identified in Cormac's *Glossary*. The name is derived from the Welsh *awen* (often translated as 'poetic inspiration' or 'mantic inspiration',[52]) and is generally conferred on a person engaged in ecstatic ritual.

> These people become rapt in an ecstasy, in which they deliver themselves of speech which is not easily intelligible because the utterances are veiled, and apparently contradictory and highly figurative. Often such people have to be shaken violently before they can recover their normal condition.[53]

In Giraldus' description, the *Awenyddion* are said to be possessed. In the early stages of their trance they are said to become hysterical and incoherent. Giraldus records that 'they roar out violently, are rendered beside themselves, and become, as it were, possessed by a spirit'.[54]

This description is very similar to Alledjenu spirits in the Bori religion. When possessed, the 'person is so strongly affected that he becomes as if insane'.[55] In many cases, individuals who have been possessed need to be shaken violently in order to return them to their bodies. The 'roaring' of the *Awenyddion*, together with the garbled speech and so on recall to mind the *fordorcha* or 'dark speech' of the poets. This is akin to secret 'spirit' languages many shamans must learn in order to commune with the ancestors. Rasmussen notes that in acquiring helping spirits, the Inuit shaman must 'not use ordinary human speech, but only the special and sacred shaman's language which he has learned from his instructor'.[56]

Such examples of ecstatic practice in a ritual context must support the thesis of Celtic shamanism. In the case of *dichetal do chennaib*, *tenm laida* and the *Awenyddion*, chant appears to be the vehicle for entering the other world. In *imbas forosnai*, ritual darkness, chewing and chanting all appear to feature. There is also some evidence for the use of entheogens in the latter example, which may point towards a variance in how *imbas* is sought.

Cultural parallels within and outwith the Celtic sphere show that ecstatic trance is a very common feature in the shamanic world. In the case of the *Awenyddion* and in *dichetal do chennaib*, we see this practice surviving into the Christian period, showing that ecstatic techniques may be fostered by a number of spiritual movements.

In each of these examples, such spiritual techniques may only be practiced by those who have received specific training. The *filidh* are said to be masters of *imbas forosnai*, *tenm laida* and *dichetal do chennaib*, implying that their tutoring is highly specialist. Without a shamanic vocabulary (mantic, ecstatic etc) it would be difficult to describe and classify these practices –

despite what Conan Doyle says, sometimes the most obvious and convenient answer *is* the correct one.

Uses of Shamanic Consciousness

The most common functions of the trance state for the shaman are the benefits of communion with the spirits of the otherworld, together with the prophetic revelations such a relationship affords. However, these are not the only purposes for entering such a condition. A shaman may become enraptured in the ecstasies of spirit for the purposes of prophecy, or for the contradictory functions of healing and harming. In the process of *imbas forosnai*, and in the ecstasy of the *Awenyddion* we have already seen examples of the former. It is to the diametrically opposed work of healing and harming that we must now focus our attention.

In Mogh Roith, we have already seen an example of the Celtic warrior shaman. Such displays of spiritual battle prowess are not restricted to his tale however. Another example is given in Tacitus's account of the invasion of Mona, which he reports may have been a druid sanctuary. When the Roman governor, Suetonius Paulinus, and his forces, arrive on the shore, they are confronted with what appears to be an ecstatic ritual to invoke fear in the enemy.

> On the shore stood the opposing army with its dense array of armed warriors, while between the ranks dashed women in black attire like the Furies, with their hair dishevelled, waving brands. All around, the druids, lifting up their hands to heaven and pouring forth dreadful imprecations, scared our soldiers by the unfamiliar sight, so that, as if their limbs were paralyzed, they stood motionless and exposed to wounds.[57]

It is not clear from the above description if the women are also druids – although history records that a druid may be of either sex. In either case, both appear to be performing the same function – stirring up their forces into a shamanic ecstasy and paralysing the opposing forces in fear.

This shamanic performance can be seen elsewhere, perhaps most notably in the *berserkirs* of Norse tradition. In times of inter-tribal conflict, the shaman is often required to intercede spiritually on their tribe's behalf – battles being won oftentimes according to whose shaman is the most effective. We see this theme also in *Forbhais Droma Dámhgháire*, where Cormac's initial gains in Munster are attributed to the superiority of his druids.

High King Cormac was said to have been murdered through the magic of druids. In some versions of this tale, he is killed because he refuses to worship their gods; in others it is because he refuses to worship *them* as gods.[58] This ambiguity is interesting from a shamanic point of view, as the ability to kill or cure would often inflate the shaman's standing and ego. Trevarthen takes this point a stage further, inferring that the druids may have been acting as oracles for their deities, and therefore in speech one becomes inseparable from the other.[59]

A stronger candidate for trance possession comes in the form of Cú Chulainn's *riastraid*, or 'battle frenzy'. All the Ulster warriors are described as being able to enter *ferg*, described as 'battle rage'. However, only Cú Chulainn is depicted as entering a state called *riastraid*.

> His *riastrad* gives him power in combat and in some cases power over animals, like the swans and deer he ties to his chariot after he kills his first men. Like the possessed Kwakiutl *hamatsa*, he is only restored to reason by immersion in tubs of water and exposure to naked women.[60]

We must see, in Cú Chulainn's battle frenzy, a quality removed from the ordinary battle fury depicted in the sources. At the start of entering this trance, Cú Chulainn shakes violently. In Kimbanguist tradition, to shake is a sign of possession – a sign that one has been chosen by the god.[61] A similar sensation is reported at the beginning of Vodou trance possession.

To gain a fuller account of *riastraid*, we must look at its description in detail. For this, I have used O'Rahilly's translation. After he begins to shake, Cú Chulainn's body begins to contort into unnatural shapes.

> Then his first distortion came upon Cu Chulainn so that he became horrible, many-shaped, strange and unrecognisable. His haunches shook about him like a tree in a current … every limb and every joint, every end and every member of him from head to foot. He performed a wild feat of contortion with his body inside his skin. His feet and his shins and his knees came to the back; his heels and his calves and his hams came to the front … He sucked one of his eyes into his head so that a wild crane could hardly have reached it to pluck it out from the back of his skull … His mouth was twisted back fearsomely. He drew the cheek back from the jawbone until the inner gullet was seen. His lungs and his liver fluttered in his mouth and throat … the torches of the war goddess … were seen in the clouds and in the air above his head with the seething of fierce rage that rose above him … The divine light rose from his forehead…[62]

There are two important points to note here. Firstly, Cú Chulainn's body becomes distorted by supernatural means. A clear indication of whether or not something is happening in spiritual reality is if it couldn't possibly happen in physical reality. This is consistent with shamanic possession descriptions. One Polynesian account describes a case of possession in a similar way:

As soon as the god was supposed to have entered the priest, the latter became violently agitated, and worked himself up to the highest pitch of apparent frenzy, the muscles of the limbs convulsed, the body swelled, the countenance became terrific, the features distorted, and the eyes wild and strained.[63]

A similar process is also seen in Australian shamanism, as part of the shamanic initiation ceremony.[64]

The second point to note from the description of Cú Chulainn's battle frenzy is the appearance of the war goddess around Cú Chulainn. The 'seething rage' produced from the goddess's torches are first described as surrounding him, and then transfers to his forehead. This implies that the spirit of the goddess herself has taken possession of his body, allowing the 'divine light' to rise within him.

It appears that the quality of Cú Chulainn's battle frenzy, unique to him and quite separate from the *ferg* or 'battle fury' of the Ulstermen, is indicative of trance possession. Mogh Roith becomes similarly distorted in his shamanic battles. Such phenomena appear to be the sole province of shamanic societies, and of shamans in particular. Taken together with his totemic name and his frequent visits to the spirit world, we may begin to speak meaningfully of Cú Chulainn as a Celtic shaman.

o0o

Shamanic healing appears to be an activity more in evidence in later Gaelic traditions than specifically primal Celtic sources. Despite this, however, some clues may reside within the function of herbs and natural cures. Davis and others have commented upon the precise knowledge of medicinal and hallucinogenic plants that some South American shamans appear to possess. While healing with herbs is not the exclusive preserve of the shaman, it becomes so when this knowledge is deemed to be given to them directly from the spirits.[65]

Such knowledge is implied in a vignette in the *Cath Maige Tuiread*. Miach, son of Dían Cécht the physician, magically heals Nuadu by replacing his lost arm with one made of silver. He subsequently replaces this one with one made of flesh. Dían Cécht grows jealous of his son's abilities, and kills him. On his grave grow three-hundred and sixty-five different healing herbs – later arranged by Airmid (his sister) according to their particular properties and uses. Dían Cécht's jealousy again betters him, and he scatters the herbs so that no one will know what they are for, 'unless Spirit showed them later'.[66]

One term used to describe druid healers in ancient texts is *fáithliaig*, which appears to combine both root words for 'healer' and 'seer'. This marries well with Pliny the Elder's depiction of druids as 'diviner and physician' as quoted in the introduction. These druid doctors were said to have knowledge of medicinal and magical herbs, as well as other sorts of treatment.[67]

o0o

Other than communion with the spirits, we can see that the Celtic shamans would also have used their powers for a number of other purposes. This range of abilities is concomitant with depictions of shamans in traditional cultures. Eliade describes the profession as encompassing the role of doctor, magician, psychopomp, priest, mystic, poet and miracle worker – amongst other traits.[68]

In considering the shamanism inherent within the Celtic world, we must now turn our attention to more general symptoms displayed by the communities the shaman represents. Without the support of the tribe, the shaman would become impotent. Not all ecstatics can be classified as shamans – the latter must be acknowledged as such by their respective peoples in order to work for communal benefit.

A Culturally Supported Schizophrenia?

In traditional cultures, the shaman will not typically define themselves as such. Instead, they find their identification through the will of their particular tribe or community. Harner encapsulates this very succinctly in the following narrative, quoted by Trevarthen:

> When anthropologist Michael Harner was studying with the South American Jívaro tribe, he noticed a man who was always in the jungle talking with spirits. He asked one of his Jívaro informants if the man was a shaman. 'No,' came the response, 'he's crazy.'[69]

This reveals two important aspects. Firstly, that 'bicameralism' (that is the phenomenon of spiritual beings talking to or through human beings in the form of visual or auditory hallucinations[70]) is not, of itself, a prerequisite of shamanism or shamanic activities. A cornerstone of shamanism is the ability of the practitioner to bring the spirits and totemic entities under their individual control; that such energies and phenomenon may be harnessed for the good of the many. The ultimate aim of such a relationship is to lead the individual to a greater effectiveness in material reality; the man in the jungle above is permanently in the spirit world, and therefore exhibits a lack of control, bringing no benefit to his people.

Secondly, we see that the culture behind the above individual's experiences must recognise the 'shaman' before this label may be applied. In short, the shaman must have the support and recognition of their respective peoples in order to be classified as such.

In Celtic sources, we can see this in two different ways: in *active* and *passive* forms of recognition. Active recognition can be seen in *Aithed Muirne re Dubh Ruis*, where the proclamation by the King of Munster specifies that Mis is to be 're-civilised' rather than punished in recognition of her 'spiritual condition'.

We can also see this in Fiacha's plea to the druid Mogh Roith in *Forbhais Droma Dámhgháire*, in acknowledgement of his superior powers. Examples of active recognition are numerous in the vernacular literature, the above two being indicative of their nature.

Passive recognition is more difficult to pin down, and relates to the tribal mentality itself rather than the shaman specifically. As mentioned in the introduction, shamanic cultures generally adopt an animistic world-view – one which finds the Sacred in all existence. This world-view (present in Celtic society, as seen earlier) complements the work of the shaman, who interacts with the spirits in many forms. We also find totemism and manism as significant (although not necessarily universal) traits found in traditional shamanic cultures. Both of these ideologies enhance the work of the shaman within their tribe, allowing their people a deeper understanding of the specific duties their shamans perform.

Perhaps the most famous example of totemism within a shamanic context can be found in the North American traditions. The tribe itself has a totem (social or collective totemism), symbolic of that particular group. In addition, each individual has a personal totem (not just the shaman, who may have many totems) which is unique to themselves.

> The guardian spirit is sometimes referred to by native North Americans as the *power animal*, as among the Coast Salish and the Okanagon of Washington. This is a particularly apt term, for it emphasizes the power-giving aspect of the guardian spirit as well as the frequency with which it is perceived as an animal. But the Coast Salish also sometimes refer to the guardian spirit as the *Indian*, for it can appear to them in human form as well. Such an animal-human duality of the guardian spirit is a common feature of North and South American Indian cosmology as well as elsewhere in the primitive world.[71]

We can see a duality between tribal and personal totemism in primal Celtic culture also. Matthews, in researching totemism within Celtic tribes, identified a number which take their names from local words for animals. Amongst his findings were:

> The Epidii of Kintyre (Horse-People), the Caerini and Lugi in Sutherland (People of the Sheep and People of the Raven), the Cornavii of Caithness (People of the Horn – as in horned animal), as well as the Tochrad (Boar People), Cattraighe (Cat Folk), Gamanrad (Stork People), Taurisci (Bull Folk), and the Brannovices (Raven Folk). These were surely at one time clan totems, if not the power animals which guarded and guided the people of each group.[72]

The quantity of such examples shows that this practice was a wide-spread phenomenon, that many tribes would identify with a particular 'totemic' animal spirit.

In addition to this, we know from earlier accounts that specific individuals within the tribe would also have individual totem spirits, unique to themselves. Cú Chulainn, for example, has a dog totem – inherent within his name – a totem which prohibited him from eating its flesh. Fraser notes that the totems are sacred to those concerned: 'The rules not to kill or eat the totem are not the only taboos; the clansmen are often forbidden to touch the totem or any part of it, and sometimes they may not even look at it.'[73] We can also see examples of individual totems in Sabha and Oisin in the Fionn tales, as discussed earlier. Totemism is a wide-spread philosophy, found among Pacific Islanders, Australian Aborigines and North American tribes; and was formerly prevalent throughout Europe, Africa and Asia.

A totem animal performs a number of functions: as a source of spiritual power; as an intermediary with the spirit world; as a spirit helper invoked to perform specific functions and so on. Many cultures, including some Pacific Island and Native

American tribes, chose to commemorate and give reference to this relationship in the form of totem poles – structures depicting both tribal totems and important ancestral figures.

This custom leads us on to a second feature commonly found in shamanic cultures: manism, or ancestor worship. The importance of manism is easy to understand when contextualised: many shamans (especially among the Rocky Mountain tribes of North America; Siberia and some Fijian tribes[74]) gain their spiritual powers through hereditary means. In addition to these examples,

> The profession of medicine man is hereditary among the Zulu and the Bechuana of South Africa, the Nyima of the southern Sudan, the Negritos and the Jakun of the Malay Peninsula, the Batak and other peoples of Sumatra, the Dyak, the sorcerers of the New Hebrides, and in several Guianan and Amazonian tribes (Shipibo, Cobeno, Macusi etc.)[75]

To this end, Eliade specifically linked the ancestor cult to the shaman, citing that the relationship with shamanic power and the ancestral spirits necessitated due reverence and respect.[76] Again this is a religious practice which can be traced in Celtic source material also.

> These customs flourished among the Celts, and, taken in connection with the reverence for the sepulchres of the dead, they point to a worship of ancestral spirits as well as of great departed heroes. Heads of the slain were offered to the 'strong shades' – the ghosts of tribal heroes whose praises were sung by bards. When such heads were placed on houses, they may have been devoted to the family ghosts. The honour in which mythic or real heroes were held may point to an actual cult, the hero being worshipped when dead, while he still continued his guardianship of the tribe.[77]

From the archaeological record, we know that the tomb of King Cottius in the Alps, for example, was a sacred place. In addition, Irish kings were often inaugurated on ancestral burial cairns, and there are numerous references associating the Irish deities with burial sites. Green notes 'the accompaniment of such [human] remains by grave-goods other than items of apparel implies a positive ritual concerning death'.[78]

We know from contemporary classical sources such as Lucan, Caesar and Diodorus Siculus that the Celts held the soul to be immortal, and that after a period of time a spirit may become reincarnated.[79] This belief is reinforced by the shaman's ability to continually cross into the spirit world and return – the shaman's role represents a microcosm of traditional Celtic cosmology.

These aspects of traditionally shamanic societies, namely animism, manism and totemism, serve to compliment the role of the shaman. Given these tools of metaphysical understanding, the tribe is able to support the duties of the shaman; just as the shaman supports and enhances the effectiveness of the tribe in the material existence.

It is these features of early tribal cultures which have given rise to theories such as those put forward by Silverman: that the shaman is a culturally supported schizophrenic.[80] To Silverman, the experience of psycho-spiritual loss encountered by the shaman in a pre-ecstatic state is comparable to 'a person undergoing schizophrenic change ... an attempt to cope with what is essentially a failure at being human – a failure at being anything one could respect as worth being'.[81] Thankfully, in this instance, anthropology has moved on somewhat since the sixties, and is now able to look more clearly at the experiential nature of the shamanic condition, without such prejudices and narrow-minded views.

Finding a Language

Our study into primal Celtic shamanism leaves just one last aspect to explore. Having discovered firstly what the Celtic shaman would have looked like, together with what their functions would have been within their communities; we must now consider how the Celtic languages would have understood this role. In finding the shamanic language in Old Irish, we must revisit some traditional translations, and perhaps propose new alternatives which encompass a more complete and accurate description of concepts which are not easily transferable into English.

To this end, we must first look at the word *dán*. The multifarious definitions for *dán* given by the Royal Irish Academy points toward an obscurity in meaning; the transmission of a concept not readily absorbed in the English language. Given variously to mean 'poetry', 'art' or 'a gift' in the material sense as in a gift of silver (*dán airgid*),[82] it also means a 'skill' in the poetic, artistic, scientific or professional sense – or the product of that skill, in the form of a poem or a song.

Another meaning of *dán* is as a 'gift' in the spiritual sense, for example either from God to man, or from man to God. Lastly, it is also given to mean something akin to 'fate' or 'destiny', as in the phrase *i ndán ocus i tairngire,* 'it was fated and foretold'.[83]

Given all of these meanings, Trevarthen has speculated that *dán* could be more correctly translated as 'co-creative power',[84] which she believes to encapsulate the basic essence of the word. I would say that this is correct, from a limited point of view, as it neglects the practical applications behind the word. *Dán*, from a more rounded point of view, could be taken to mean either 'shamanism' or 'the shamanic condition'.

Where this meaning is most evident is in the sense of *dán* as a spiritual gift: a gift from God to man, or a gift from man to

God.[85] This displays an interaction with spiritual forces which is the foundation principle of shamanic activity: as Kalweit describes shamanism as both a *personal* and *interactive* contact with the Sacred. In this sense, *dán* can be seen to represent that interaction.

We can see how this is put into practical effect in the Old Irish tales. The god Lugh is given the epithet *Samildánach* – traditionally translated as 'many skilled' or 'all skilled'. When Lugh arrives at Tara in the *Cath Maige Tuired*, the doorkeeper asks: 'What art do you practice? For no one without an art enters Tara' (*Cia dán frisa ng[n]éte? Al séi, 'ar ni téid nech cin dán i Temruid'*).[86] In response to this, Lugh informs the doorkeeper that he possesses all skills, including supernatural ones. *Samildánach*, as the condition of possessing all skills combined with supernatural knowledge could signify the position of the shaman within the community.

This translation is supported by a number of other factors. Firstly, Amergin's song quoted in the previous section in reference to shamanic costuming and transformations is called *dán* – an expression of his shamanic capabilities. Secondly, the word *dán* also appears in the title *Áes Dána*, or 'people of art'. The *Áes Dána* are characterised by their work with spirits (as in the case of the *lucht cumachtai* or 'people of power'), but are also associated with the spirits themselves in some accounts. For example, *Echtra Cormaic* clearly associates the *Áes Dána* with the *Áes Síd*, or 'spirit people'. This ambiguity between the material and the spiritual is representative of the shamanic mindset.

Finally, the *Tuatha Dé Dánnan* also have the word *dán* in their name. Often translated as 'tribe of the Goddess Danu' or similar, this phrase could actually mean 'tribe of the God-Song' or 'tribe of the Song of God'. Many shamanic cultures think of singing as a spiritual interaction. In describing methods of shamanic recruitment among the Altaians and Buryat, Eliade notes: 'during his ecstasy the candidate sings shamanic hymns. This is a sign that contact with the beyond has finally been established.'[87] We know from the old bardic traditions that – to the Celts – poetry and song are inextricably linked. The modern English word 'poetry' comes from the Greek verb *poieein*, meaning 'to make'; thus poetry is a creative act. This links in with the notion of primal, creative song as described in Iolo Morgannwg's *Barddas* quoted in an earlier chapter. It is interesting to think that it is through poetry and song in the form of the Gaelic oral tradition that shamanic elements of Celtic spirituality have survived in Celtic regions – the focus of section three of this book.

Wrapped up in *dán* are notions of fate and destiny – concepts which reflect the nature of the shaman's 'call to vocation' by the spirits. We have already seen that *dán* is associated with this spiritual interaction, and therefore we see how strongly it resembles the shamanic mould.

In all of these definitions, I believe we can find one seed. The shaman's duties cover many skills and arts; they must be able to interact freely with the spiritual powers and work in ways which benefit their tribe. In *dán*, we find a word which encapsulates this varied and multifaceted concept. In its practical use, we find it reflects the shamanic functions which we have found in primal Celtic society, which supports the translation of *dán* as the Celtic version of 'shamanism' offered above. The *Áes Dána*, so often encountered in early Irish literature, therefore, are the 'shamans' whose work supports and profits their respective tribes.

o0o

It is important to note, before we move on to modern *Gàidhlig* traditions and folklore, that many of the interpretations and translations given in the preceding sections are representative of a certain point of view. For some of this material, there are equally plausible explanations and interpretations which Celticists have agreed upon in mainstream academia. However, despite this, I believe that a shamanic interpretation is the only way to understand sufficiently *all* of the material presented in the previous two sections, and provides a basis for understanding the resulting traditions and practices which have grown from their roots.

PART THREE

A SHAMAN IN THE GÀIDHEALTACHD ?

We don't sing the songs anymore. And when we don't sing the songs, the animals soon leave. That what we doin' to the world: lettin' nature go off to die. Because we don't sing the songs.

Aboriginal informant to James Cowan in *The Aborigine Tradition*

The Voice of the Elements

Mar a bha, mar a tha   As it was, as it is
Mar a bhitheas gu brath   As it ever shall be
Ri traghadh 's ri lionadh   With the ebb and the flow
Mar a bhitheas gu brath.   As it ever shall be.

Traditional Song Fragment

Embedded within the Gaelic oral tradition, we can find the successors of the shamanism, the *dánach*, inherent within more primal Celtic sacred practice. Many scholars now recognise that a number of pagan elements have survived into these later traditions; such as the presence of water divinities, or *gainisg*, which Carmichael describes in his glossary as 'a small divinity dwelling among reeds and marshes on the borders of lakes and banks of rivers, moaning and wailing before storms for the deaths that are to follow'.[1] These are most likely folk memories of local divinities and spirits which were numinous throughout Celtic areas.[2]

In addition, heroes and gods from pagan Celtic mythology continue to appear and are worshipped in the Christian period. Brigit is perhaps the most famous example of these, serving as a Celtic Saint whose religious message has now been 'altered' to reflect the ideologies behind a new spiritual movement.

Recognising, then, that some pagan elements have survived into the Christian period; it is reasonable to assume that their mode of practice (shamanism) may also have withstood a concomitant endurance.

Our first evidence for this comes within the structure of, and philosophy behind, the modern Gaelic language. As we have already seen, an animistic world-view often goes hand-in-hand with shamanistic consciousness. This world-view is expressed in the way Scots Gaelic allows certain phrases to be framed. This is best shown via expressions of possession.

In modern Scots Gaelic it is not possible to say *mo duine* ('my man' or 'my husband'), one must say *an duine agam* (literally, 'the man that is at me'). This construction removes any notion of possession: in Gaelic, one is not defined by one's relationships. This construction extends to a number of other things, for example *an char agam* (literally, 'the car that is at me'); *an chu agam* ('the dog that is at me') etc. In order to express one's occupation, one must say *'s e leabharleannach a th'annam* (literally, 'it's a librarian that's within me'). Again, this construction removes the personal pronoun from the descriptive word.

Finally, one cannot be defined by one's emotions. In Gaelic, in order to express fear, one must say *tha an t-eagal orm* ('a fear is upon me'). Interestingly, the verb 'to be' is derived from the Old Irish *ta*, meaning 'to stand'. Therefore, when expressing personal information, one must say 'I stand…' rather than 'I am…' again removing any sense of permanence.

So what can you say *mo*/'my' for in Gaelic? You can say *mo lamh* ('my hand') as that is an element which is inalienable from the self. Similarly, you can say *m'anam* ('my spirit') for a similar reason. Blood family are also described in this way, as they cannot be removed from the essential makeup of the self. Finally, it is possible to use the term *mo* when speaking religiously. For example, *mo Dhé* or *mo Bhrighide* ('my God' or 'my Brigit' etc). This shows that spirit, family and divinity are qualities which are completely inalienable from the self in Gaelic – qualities which are completely in accord with an animistic world view. The removal of materialism from the language reveals a more spiritual mode of consciousness, one which has survived from Old Irish expressions and structures.

The animistic elements of Gaelic spirituality are also in evidence within the oral tradition itself. An example of this can be seen in a prayer entitled *Guth na Torainn* or 'the Voice of Thunder'. As we have seen, an animistic world-view recognises a life within natural phenomenon. This is expressed in *Guth na Torainn*:

A Dhé nan dùla,	Oh God of the elements,
A Dhé nan rùna,	Oh God of the mysteries,
A Dhé nan rùla,	Oh God of the stars,
A Rìgh nan rìgh !	Oh King of kings !
A Rìgh nan rìgh !	Oh King of kings !
Do shonas an sonas,	Thy joy, the joy,
Do sholas an solas,	Thy light, the light,
Do chogadh an cogadh,	Thy war, the war,
Do shìth an t-sìth	Thy peace, the peace
Do shìth an t-sìth	Thy peace, the peace
Do chràdh an cràdh,	Thy pain, the pain,
Do ghràdh an gràdh,	Thy love, the love,
A mhaireas gu bràth	That lasts for aye,
Gu crìoch nan crìoch,	To the end of ends,
Gu crìoch nan crìoch,	To the end of ends.[3]

Of this prayer, the reciter said 'the old people had runes which they sang to the spirits dwelling in the sea and in the mountain, in the wind and in the whirlwind, in the lightning and in the thunder, in the sun and in the moon and in the stars of heaven'.[4] In this religious practice we see a reinforcement of the animistic philosophy: the elements, the stars etc. are all equated with divine experience. Even abstract concepts such as 'love', 'war' and 'light' are equated with God. In animistic philosophies, nothing can be separate from the Sacred, as all things are alive and, in some sense, divine.

In this third section, I will look at the Gaelic oral tradition and folklore. In the case of the former, my principle source will be the *Carmina Gadelica* compiled by Alexander Carmichael in the latter half of the nineteenth, and early years of the twentieth centuries. Encompassing six volumes, Carmichael's dictations and notes are by far the most comprehensive of such studies of the traditions, and are a rich source for shamanism within the Gàidhealtachd.

In our search for the shaman in the Gàidhealtachd, it is possible to see a progression in religious and spiritual ideologies. In pagan times, the multiplicity of deity names points towards a polytheistic set of beliefs. In later times, when such philosophies were increasingly persecuted by later religious groups, we can see a movement toward a more henotheistic attitude – the belief in the Christian God without necessarily denying the existence of other, more local deities. This is a belief structure very much in evidence in other Christian colonies, and has given rise to many spiritual bodies such as Santeria and certain other Vodou communities.

In the western isles, I believe it is true to say that the more primal connections with spirits and deities never truly died out. As one modern day practitioner of druidry has explained:

> To question whether the tradition has an unbroken history reveals a misunderstanding about what Druidry is. As the relationship between the people and the land, set within a language of honour and spiritual respect, it not only allows, even encourages, but also requires us to adapt each and every teaching to the perfect relevance of the situation we are experiencing, here and now. Druidry could not be lost.[5]

In these following chapters, I hope the abundance of material in support of this attitude will highlight the truth behind its assertions.

Riochd nan Daoine

At the beginning of this study we looked at the shamanic costume as a microcosm of the shamanic consciousness. The animal and spiritual symbolism adopted by the shaman represent the ability to enter into a trance consciousness; to cross the boundaries between material and spiritual existences. The shaman is able to do this at will; when the shaman is wearing his ritual costuming and carrying his shamanic gear it is a signal that he is operating within a shamanic consciousness, outside of normal material reality.

In a persecuted culture, outward signs of shamanic activity become increasingly difficult to adopt. Any visible indication of shamanic activity under a Christian regime would be met immediately with derision and scorn. A similar dilemma has recently beset the Tuvan community, who have been forced to relinquish any public displays of shamanism under Russian supervision.[6]

Despite this, however, we do find scraps of evidence to show that shamanic costuming and instrumentation is still in evidence in later Gaelic speaking areas. For example, Johnson's tour of the Hebrides in the late eighteenth century reveals a peculiar custom on a visit the island of Coll:

> Mr. *Maclean* informed us of an odd game, of which he did not tell the original, but which may perhaps be used in other places, where the reason is not yet forgot. At New-year's eve, in the hall or castle of the Laird, where, at festal seasons, there may be supposed a very numerous company, one man dresses himself in a cow's hide, upon which other men beat with sticks. He runs with all this noise around the house, which all the company quits in a counterfeited fright: the door is then shut. At New-year's eve there is no great pleasure to be had out of doors in the *Hebrides*. They are sure soon to recover from their terror enough to solicit for re-admission; which, for the honour of poetry, is not to be obtained but by repeating a verse, with which those that are knowing and provident take care to be furnished.[7]

Johnson's description sounds very much like an early contender for the Hallowe'en tradition of 'trick or treat'.[8] Dressing in animal hides, however, and impersonating a bull, may have a more shamanic significance, of which the above game may be a half-remembered version.

Among the Yakut, the bull is thought to be one of the most powerful *ié-kyla*, or spirit totems.[9] Harner notes that:

> The belief by shamans that they can metamorphose into the form of their guardian animal spirit or power animal is widespread and obviously ancient... In northernmost Scandinavia, Lapp shamans changed into wolves, bears, reindeer, and fish, and Siberian and Eskimo shamans frequently transformed themselves into wolves.[10]

As we have already seen, the thinking behind wearing animal costuming for the shaman is to 'become' the animal itself: *one becomes what one displays.* As far as Harner is concerned, this belief survived in Europe at least until the Renaissance, but possibly later still.

> The Christian Church, of course, considered persons engaged in animal metamorphosis to be wizards, witches, and sorcerers, and persecuted them through the Inquisition. Yet a colleague of Gallileo, the alchemist and scientist Giovanni Battista Porta, in 1562 still possessed the ancient knowledge of how to experience such a metamorphosis and published the information in his famous book, *Natural Magick*. Thus he explains how, using a hallucinogenic potion, a man would 'believe he has changed into a Bird or a Beast'.[11]

In Porta's account, he observed that certain individuals engaged in these activities would 'seem sometimes to be changed into a fish; and flinging out his arms, would swim on the Ground'; or another would believe himself to be turned into a goose 'and would eat Grass, and beat the Ground with his Teeth, like a Goose: now and then sing, and endeavour to clap his Wings'.[12]

The *Book of Arran* records an interesting piece of folklore from this area which may also represent a continuation of animal costuming, describing a woman who appeared to have hooves instead of feet. The hoofed woman was said to be able to outrun an ordinary person, and ate raw animal flesh[13] – reminiscent of the Kwakiutl *hamatsa* cannibal dancer mentioned in relation to the *gelta* earlier.

Returning to the Gaelic oral tradition, the *Ora Ceartas*, or invocation for justice, performed before going into court, lists a number of animal forms which the reciter is able to assume in order to make them more powerful than 'all persons'.

> *Is dubh am bail ud thall, is dubh daoine th'ann;*
> *Is mis an eala bhan, Banruinn os an ceann.*
> *Falbhaidh mi an ainme Dhé,*
> *an riochd feidh, an riochd each*
> *an riochd nathrach, an riochd righ:*
> *Is treason lion fin na le gach neach.*
>
> Dark is yonder town, dark those therein;
> I am the white swan, Queen above them.
> I will go in the name of God,
> in likeness of deer, in likeness of horse,
> in likeness of Serpent, in likeness of King:
> Stronger will it be with me than with all persons.[14]

This invocation reveals the relationship between the shaman and the totem: the shaman may 'become' a certain animal in order to imbue himself spiritually with that animal's attributes. The reference to the 'white swan, Queen above them' shows that this represents the superiority of the shaman above the profane.

A number of shamanic totems, or spirit animals, are named in the *Book of Arran* in relation to certain families. MacKenzie lists twenty-one different families and their associated totems, known in Gaelic as *riochd* or 'dream signs'. In relating an argument between two women, a Currie and a MacGregor, MacKenzie relates that the Currie woman asked '*Dé thug na coin-dhubha dh'Arainn?*' (What brought the blood-hounds to

Arran?). The MacGregor woman answered '*Thàinig oad a riagadh na feadagan a Lag-na-moine*' (They came to hunt the plovers out of Lag-na-moine). MacKenzie explains that 'the 'riochd' of a Macgregor was the bloodhound, that of a Currie the plover'.[15] For the sake of illustration, the 'dream signs' recorded by the *Book of Arran* are included below:

MacGregors	bloodhounds.	MacKelvies	doves.
MacAlisters	sheep dogs.	MacDonalds	sheep dogs.
Curries	plovers.	MacKenzies	bees.
MacNicols	cats.	Cooks	pigs, bulls.
Hamiltons	hares	Kerrs	sheep
MacLardys	asses.	MacNeils	dun bull.
Bannatynes	mice.	MacMillans	wood-pigeons.
Robertsons	rats.	Fullartons	geese.
Stewarts	lions?	MacMasters	pigs.
MacKinnons	rabbits.	MacNeishes	cats.
Sillars	frogs.[16]		

The above *riochd* or 'dream signs' of particular families represent the inheritance of the tribal totem – in shamanic societies it was often prohibited for members of the same tribe to marry, a custom repeated in many Scottish communities.

Ross tells us that the MacIntoshes were known as *Clan Chattan*. In the fourteenth century, they owned the greater part of Badenoch; the cat was their crest and their motto: 'Touch not the cat gloveless'.[17] In addition to this, superstition has it that before a member of the Breadalbane family died, a bull would be heart at night roaring on a hillside. Such death-signs may also reveal a totemic relationship.

Shamanic totems do not have to be animals, however, and there is some ephemeral evidence to suggest that plants may have qualified for this interpretation in the Gaidhealtachd also:

> The MacDonalds, for example, wore heather, which was their war-cry (fraoch); the Grants fir (giuthas); the MacIntoshes holly (cuileann). To a certain extent the

choice of badge would be determined by what was available in a given locality, but it is likely that the chosen plant would also have a magical and evil-averting significance.[18]

It is interesting to note the inclusion of a number of avian totems: 'dove', 'wood-pigeon', and so on. As we have seen, numerous occurrences of avian symbolism in ritual costuming has led to the bird being seen as the shamanic totem *par excellence* – a concept which we have found to be replicated in primal Celtic culture. We also find an abundance of shamanic material concerning flight and bird imitation in later Gaelic folklore and traditions.

The Language of Birds

C *ànain* *nan* *Eun*, a traditional later Scottish tale, demonstrates how profoundly Gaelic shamanism was associated with birds. The 'Island of the Birds' features in a number of older Celtic tales including the voyages of Máelduin and Brendan. In *Cànain nan Eun*, Alasdair's father wants to give his son the best education possible, and accordingly sends him to the 'Isle of Birds' in order to learn their language. Each time Alasdair returns from the island, his father asks him what he has learned. After the first year, Alasdair replies 'I can see'. After two years, he replies 'I can see and I can hear'. After three years, he says 'I can see, and I can hear, and I can understand'.[19]

After a chaffinch delivers a prophecy that Alasdair's father will face humiliation at his son's hands, Alasdair's father orders all of the birds killed. Alasdair returns to the island for three more years, and as the birds recognise him they flock around him. Slowly, Alasdair begins to kill and eat the birds, 'so that if he wished for any further acquaintance with bird language he got it during those three years'.[20] This is interesting as it implies that during the process of killing and consuming the birds, Alasdair was continuing to learn. Perhaps this is meant to imply that in the process of consumption, Alasdair is able to take on some of the power of the bird much in the same way that the Andaman Islanders kill and eat turtle meat during their initiation ceremonies and then dance the turtle in order to show that they have its power.[21]

In one Egyptian funerary text, the deceased is depicted as a huntsman who eats his gods and thereby gains their power and understanding. After a gory illustration of killing, dismemberment, evisceration and cooking, the deceased 'devours their hearts and crowns and thereby gains their powers, so that their magic is in his body; he swallows the understanding of every god...'[22]

During the initiation ceremony of the Samoyed shaman, the candidate is spiritually dismembered and boiled in a cauldron.

> On the fire was a cauldron 'as big as half the earth'. The naked man saw him and caught him with a huge pair of tongs. The novice had time to think, 'I am dead!'. The man cut off his head, chopped his body into bits, and put everything in the cauldron. There he boiled his body for three years.[23]

After this episode, the candidate is taught by the naked man certain elements in the nature of shamanic healing – he gains the power to correctly identify and cure shamanic illness.

In *Cànain nan Eun*, Alasdair undergoes an ordeal similar to that of Mis: both their hair and nails grow long. Despite his appearance, Alasdair is adopted by a ship's captain and is able to use his knowledge of bird language to solve a king's long standing problem with some ravens. He marries a princess and appears to have returned to civilisation, but ultimately his feral state returns.

Alasdair is restored to beauty by bathing in the blood of three children. The children, whose throats had been cut, are then miraculously cured and returned to life, suggesting that Alasdair's return to civilisation is akin to a return to life. We have seen that the initiation ordeals a shaman must undergo typically involve some form of suffering, death, and subsequent resurrection.

The tale concludes with Alasdair becoming king in his own land. The chaffinch's prophecy is fulfilled when Alasdair's father sets his teeth to a knot in the king's shoelace and his mother stands with a basin. Alasdair's father says it would be just to slay him. He responds, 'There is no knowing whether I should ever have been king had not everything happened as it has, but never again shall you need alms.'

In this story, the 'Isle of the Birds' appears to represent the spirit world, where Alasdair learns how to see, to hear and to understand – in short, he learns everything. Various traditional cultures express both 'magic' and 'bird song' in similar terms. For example, the Germanic word for magical incantations is *galdr*, from the verb *galan* ('to sing') – a term specifically applied to bird song. Also the Latin term *carmen* denotes both a 'spell' and a 'song' or 'poem'.

Eliade qualifies Alasdair's relationship with the birds as the utopia of the world before the fall.

> In numerous traditions friendship with animals and understanding their language represent paradisal syndromes. In the beginning, that is, in mythical times, man lived at peace with the animals and understood their speech. It was not until after a primordial catastrophe, comparable for the 'Fall' of Biblical tradition, that man became what he is today – mortal, sexed, obliged to work to feed himself, and at enmity with the animals. While preparing for his ecstasy and during it, the shaman abolishes the present human condition and, for the time being, recovers the situation as it was at the beginning.

> Friendship with animals, knowledge of their language, transformation into an animal are many signs that the shaman has re-established the 'paradisal' situation lost at the dawn of time.[24]

Like Mis and Suibhne, Alasdair goes through a feral stage. Like Mis, he is deemed extremely valuable, as the Prince of Spain sacrifices his children in order to return him to civilisation. This demonstrates a support and recognition on behalf of Alasdair's community and friends – the sacrificed children's subsequent return to life is also representative of the shaman's initiation as transcending death.

Imitation of the language of birds leads on to another practice recorded in the Gaelic oral tradition. Volume four of Alexander Carmichael's *Carmina Gadelica* opens with a chapter entitled *Beo-Chreutrairean* ('Live Creatures'), and discusses the widespread practice of animal imitations. Carmichael sites sixteen examples, of which the majority relate to birds. One poem, called *Glòir nan Eun*, or 'The Speech of Birds', records the conversation between two mavises, a corncrake, a crow, a cuckoo and a pigeon. Many of their speeches represent invocations, such as the corncrake:

A Dhia nam feart!	Oh God of the powers!
A Dhia nam feart!	Oh God of the powers!
Cuir biadh sa ghart!	Put food in the field!
Cuir biadh sa ghart!	Put food in the field![25]

The School of Scottish Studies based at Edinburgh University have recordings of some of these cries and poems. Listening to them, one is impressed at how closely each recitation resembles the song of its particular bird.

Many other tales within this volume also relate stories attributed to particular birds, but may actually have represented tales of individuals imitating a bird. The example of *conan corr* (the wren) is quoted below:

Conan Corr (the wren) went with his twelve sons to the peat moss to pull a carrot. Conan grasped the carrot by the ear, and he was stamping his soles, and he was swaying it thither and swaying it hither, plough-casting it and peat-cutting it. White was his hue and red his cheek, but never did he take away the carrot from the smooth clasps of the ground, - the fat rich carrot of the virtues and of the blessings.

'Come hither one warrior!' quoth Conan Corr. Conan and his son again grasped the carrot by the ear. They were swaying it thither and swaying it hither, and plough-casting it, and peat-cutting it.

So they did one after another, until the twelve sons took an ear-grip on the carrot. They all hauled once, and hauled twice, and hauled thrice on the ear of the carrot, and Conan and his twelve sons fell flat on their backs in the peat bog; but never did they take the ... carrot from out its firm foundation.[26]

This tale appears to be in the form of a parable, much in the same way a shaman attempts to instruct his community in moral and spiritual matters.

Birds were not the only creatures to have been given a voice in the Gaelic oral tradition. Others include the cat, dogs, seals, mice, rats, butterflies and the red fox. Eliade argues that the imitation of animal voices represents the shaman's ability to frequently cross the boundaries between the physical and spiritual realms.

Imitating animal voices, using this secret language during the séance, is yet another sign that the shaman can move freely thought the three cosmic zones: underworld, earth, sky. This is as much as to say that he can make his way safely where only the dead or the gods have access. Embodying an animal during the séance is less a possession than a magical transformation of the shaman into that animal. A similar transformation can also be obtained by other means – by donning the shamanic costume, for example, or concealing the face under a mask.[27]

According to Carmichael, the Gaels were very effective in this technique, even to the point of fooling the birds themselves.

> I have seen men and women, boys and girls, who could sing and croon and whistle imitations of birds so effectively that the birds themselves stood still and listened, turning their heads this way and that to ascertain whence the sound came, and tentatively, cautiously drawing nearer to it.[28]

It is likely that the practice of bird imitation relates to an earlier pagan Celtic practice of divination. Diodorus Siculus comments:

> The Gauls likewise make use of diviners, accounting them worthy of high approbation, and these men foretell the future by means of the flight and *cries of birds* and of the slaughter of sacred animals, and they have all the multitude subservient to them.[29]

In South America, the neophyte shaman must learn to imitate the voices of animals during his initiation period.[30] The same is true of North America. The Pomo and the Menomini shamans, amongst others, imitate bird songs.[31] Also, during the séances of the Yakut, Chukchee, Inuit, Goldi and Yugakir, wild animal and bird cries are heard during shamanic ritual.[32]

The shaman's ability to imitate bird and other cries is indicative of their ability to communicate with animals. According to Eliade, 'all over the world learning the language of animals, especially of birds, is equivalent to knowing the secrets of nature and hence to being able to prophesy'.[33]

One particular example of bird imitation in the Gaelic tradition ties it more closely to the shamanic condition. Known as *pilililiu*, and meant to imitate the cry of the redshanks bird,[34] this song was thought to be used to sing the soul of the deceased over to the spirit world. The redshanks bird is so called because of its red legs, contrasted against a white plumage. This colouring gives the bird an otherworldly quality in Celtic traditions: red and white are frequently associated with the spirits in the tales. In addition to this, the fact that the redshanks is a wader bird was thought to be significant, as this allowed it to unite the three realms of earth, sea and sky (comparable to the shaman's role in uniting the three worlds, upper, middle and lower).

A second school of thought on the *pilililiu* holds it to be an imitation of the bagpipe.[35] Whilst at first glance this may appear to undermine the above argument, it is possible that the bagpipe was used to imitate the cries of birds and other animals also. The aboriginal didgeridoo can be used for this purpose[36] – both the bagpipe and the didgeridoo are overtoning instruments. Alexander MacDonald, a piper from South Uist, was recorded by Carmichael as having verified this:

> The old pipers could play and whistle many imitations of the song of the swan, the long-tailed duck, the lark, the merle and the mavis, and other birds of our western coasts, some of them only visitors, whether of summer or of winter.[37]

The Gaelic word *seinn* appears to be descriptive of this practice. MacLennan appears to suggest that 'chant', 'warble' and 'birdsong' are all relevant interpretations of *seinn*.[38] If we apply all three meanings simultaneously, *seinn* would appear to describe the imitation of animal sounds by means of chant or song. MacLennan also adds that *seinn* can be applied to the sound made when an instrument is played (as in the bagpipe example above) and to church music. This lends *seinn* a sacred air, leading us back to the shaman.

In defining the role of the shaman, Eliade includes psychopomp – one who ushers the souls of the dead into the spirit world. The shaman is able to cross into the spirit world freely and return, meaning that this function could be performed without risk to the shaman. Perhaps in the *pilililiu*, we see a reflection of this role. The soul of the departed was thought to travel along the voice of the reciter, and by the medium of song, arrive in the spirit world without trauma or danger. In a sense, the reciter would accompany the spirit of the deceased into the otherworld by means of their voice.

ri traghadh 's ri lionadh[39]

Popular children's author Lewis Carroll once described awareness of the spiritual dimension as the 'Eerie State'. One 'in which, while conscious of actual surroundings, he is *also* conscious of the presence of Fairies'[40] – what in Gaelic tradition would be called the *dà shealladh*, or 'two-sights'.[41] Beyond the 'Eerie' state,

> ...a form of trance, in which, while unconscious of actual surroundings and apparently asleep, he (i.e. his immaterial essence) migrates to other scenes, in the actual world, or in Fairyland, and is conscious of the presence of Fairies.[42]

In shamanic cultures, as we have already seen, trance is induced by a number of means: drumming, chanting, psychotropic drugs (or entheogens) and sensory deprivation. We will look at some of the others in this list in the next chapter, however it is the latter mode (sensory deprivation) which we find in greatest abundance in later Gaelic traditions.

The *Book of Arran* discusses a well-attested practice amongst many latter day Celtic saints.

Such action, a deliberate choice of a hermit life in some remote and uninhabited isle, had of course precedents and examples enough among the Celtic saints. Isolation, semi-starvation, lacerating the body with hardship, were accounted forms of spiritual discipline ... the mode was to confine oneself in a circular stone-built hut...[43]

For the Carib shaman, usually up to six youths are initiated at the one time. Of their initiation, Eliade says: 'They live in complete isolation in a hut built especially for the purpose and covered with palm fronds. They are required to do a certain amount of manual work'.[44] In addition to this, Eliade adds 'throughout the instruction period fasting is almost absolute'.[45]

Fasting and isolation are two effective methods of inducing a trance state. In the case of the Carib shamanic candidate, fasting can last as long as twenty-four days and nights. In the case of the Celtic saints – according to the *Book of Arran* – the individual lives in 'semi-starvation' for the rest of their life.

Eliade sees the isolation and fasting of the Carib shaman as preparation for the ecstatic journey. Part of the training of these individuals includes how to turn into a number of creatures and introduces them to their guiding spirits. The ritual isolation and starvation of the Celtic saints appears to form a similar spiritual function: in so doing, the saint seeks a closer kinship with the Sacred.

Shamanic election and initiation in South America often preserves the cosmic schema of ritual death and resurrection. This ritual death is suggested through a number of means 'extreme fatigue, tortures, fasting, blows and so on'.[46] Among the Jívaro, upon deciding to become a shaman the candidate approaches a suitable master and pays him an appropriate fee. He then embarks on a severe regime of fasting and drinking narcotic beverages (particularly tobacco juice). As a result of this, the spirit Pasuka appears in the form of a warrior. Upon its appearance the master strikes the body of the neophyte until he falls to the ground unconscious – this proves that the spirit has taken possession of him and that he has undergone a ritual, spiritual death.[47]

From these intercultural parallels, we gain a better insight into the ritual starvation, isolation and hardships endured by the Celtic saints. Through a physical death, the individual (be they saint or shamanic candidate) may transcend the material condition and enter the ecstasy of spirit sought by the shaman.

oOo

Starvation and isolation are not the only means of sensory deprivation employed in later Gaelic traditions however. Prayer and penance in water in search of spiritual 'heat' also features heavily in the later Celtic hagiographies.

Prayer in water is an ascetic practice, one which was thought to reflect great piety in later Christian times. Gougaud has shown that praying whilst immersed in water was not merely a hagiographical 'motif' however. Immersion was usually practiced as a way of crushing desire and 'humiliating the body' – a precursor of the cold shower! It is often found in a penitential context, although not exclusively.[48]

The practice of immersion was often accompanied by chanting or singing (usually of the Christian psalms), and according to the sources, harsh weather conditions acted as no deterrent for this ascetic act. Although immersion in water is an international act of devotional piety, and not limited to one culture or time-period, Gougaud argues that it is characteristic of early Irish saints.

Ireland argues that this practice 'would seem to have come with monasticism from the Near East. It is recorded of the desert fathers and would seem to be common in the biblical Apocrypha'.[49] In the Irish *Saltair na Rann,* both Adam and Eve do penance after the Fall by immersing themselves up to the neck in water and praying with their arms stretched upwards in supplication.

Perhaps the oldest recorded reference to the practice in Irish tradition comes from Muirchu's *Life* of Saint Patrick (circa 680 ACE). In one episode, Patrick tested Benignus by asking him if he knew what he (Patrick) was experiencing there and then. Benignus replied that he saw heaven open and beheld the son of God and His angels. From this, Patrick recognized Benignus as his successor, and led him to his usual place of prayer – which Muirchu tells us is in the middle of a river-bed. When Benignus complained that he could no longer endure the temperature, Patrick suggested that he move from the upper to the lower river. However, Benignus found this water to be too hot, and had to resurface and sit on the shore. As Ireland argues, the sudden rise in temperature is due to Saint Patrick's 'spiritual ardour' – a feature which 'has all the signs of a highly evolved literary motif with a long history, probably cultivated in an Irish setting'.[50]

The motif of the saint's spiritual ardour heating freezing waters is found in the Lives of five different saints edited by Plummer: Saint Ciarán of Saigir, Saint Kevin of Glendalough, Saint Comgall of Bangor, Saint Fechín of Fore and Saint Laisrén of Daminis.[51] Adomnán makes no mention of the practice in the *Life* of Saint Columba, but later biographers do. In the Middle Irish *Life*, it is reported that Columba would often spend the night chanting psalms on the seashore until morning and cites a poem which says that he did so '*isin liur fri toeb Alaban*'/'in the sea alongside Scotland'.[52] The sixteenth century *Betha Coluimb Chille* says that the angels used to console him when he spent time in rough weather '*no ó beith 'n-a sesamh a nuisce gó a smeig ag radh urnaidhte rofaide a n-aimseruib geimhreta no sneachtamla*'/'standing up to his chin in water engaged in protracted prayer'.[53]

Chant appears to be a common feature in immersion. In a late Irish *Life* of Saint Magnenn of Kilmainham, Magnenn, whilst on a visit to Tallaght, found Máel Ruain 'just emerging out of a well of water after chanting of the psalter's three times fifty psalms'.[54] Likewise, in the preface to *Félire Óengusso*, it is said of Óengus that he 'used to chant his psalms thus ... to wit, fifty in the river with a withe around his neck and tied to the tree; fifty under the tree, and fifty in his cell'.[55]

We have already seen the effects of chant in a shamanic context, and will revisit them in the next chapter. Immersion in water, however, adds an extra dimension to this technique. The Tungus, Chukchee and Lapps refer to the ecstatic trance as 'immersion'.[56] The purpose of the practice appears to have been to reach a state of piety and mental clarity – one which removes physical stimulus. In this, we are reminded of the 'enlightenment' of *imbas forosnai* and similar practices, where sensory deprivation techniques are also in evidence. Immersion and prayer in water is also a feature of initiation ceremonies among Buryat shamans.[57]

The concept of 'spiritual heat' is also interesting from a shamanic context. In pan-Indian ideology *tapas*, whose original meaning is 'extreme heat', has come to be associated with ascetic effort.[58] Prajāpati creates the world by 'heating' himself to an extreme temperature through asceticism, by a means of 'magical' sweating.

> The 'inner heat' or 'mystical heat' is creative: it results in a kind of magical power that, even when not manifested directly as a cosmogony (cf. the myth of Prajāpati) 'creates' on a lesser cosmic plane; for example, it creates the countless illusions or miracles of the ascetics and yogins (magical flight, negation of physical laws, disappearance, etc.). Now, 'inner heat' forms an integral part of the technique of 'primitive' magicians and shamans.[59]

In addition to this, some Indo-Tibetan initiatory ordeals consist of testing a candidate's degree of preparation by his ability, during a winter night snow-storm, to dry a large number of soaked sheets using only the 'mystical heat' produced by his body.[60] This keys in directly to Irish practice, where oftentimes a substitute for immersion in water was sleeping in wet clothes.[61]

Such techniques are clearly shamanic in their purpose and application. The resulting 'mystical' or 'inner heat' is one which finds many parallels in the shamanic world, induced by the power of the spirits.

The practice of prayer and penance in water appears to have been most popular in the medieval period, however a possible twentieth century reference may also be included in Carmichael's *Carmina Gadelica*. In describing the way many of the chants and prayers he recorded were sung, Carmichael remembered:

> ...the people hum the prayer in an inaudible undertone peculiar to themselves, like the soft murmur of the ever-murmuring sea, like the far-distant eerie sighing of the wind among trees, or like the muffled cadence of far-away waters, rising and falling upon the fitful autumn wind.[62]

As well as imitating the calls of animals, Carmichael appears to suggest that Gaelic songs would often imitate the sound of the sea. This is perhaps in memory of the older Christian practice of prayer and penance immersed in water.

o0o

One final example of sensory deprivation in later Gaelic tradition comes from an anecdote on the life of Saint Oran. An associate of Saint Columba, Saint Oran was said to have held different beliefs to his spiritual mentor. Upon a disagreement in

99

theological matters, Saint Oran suggested that he be buried alive 'as deep down as Oran was high up',[63] and would endure in this state for three days and nights. At the end of this period, Columba ordered Oran to be exhumed. Upon opening his eyes, Saint Oran proclaimed:

> *Ni bheil flathas mar a theireas,*
> *Ni bheil trionn mar a thubhras,*
> *Ni bheil saoi suthann sona,*
> *Ni bheil daoi dona duthann.*[64]

> Nor is heaven as is alleged,
> Nor is hell as is asserted,
> Nor are the good forever happy,
> Nor are the bad forever unhappy.[65]

Upon hearing this blasphemy, Columba ordered Saint Oran to be buried again 'lest scandal should be given to the faith'.[66]

Such examples of live burial are known in shamanic cultures. Eliade concludes that one of the main features of shamanic initiations is a 'symbolic burial in the temple or fetish house'.[67] With this in mind, it is interesting to note that a chapel to Saint Oran, built where he was said to be buried, was the first Christian structure to be built on Iona.

The medicine men of the Nicobar Islands use a symbolic burial in their initiation ceremonies also.

> The relatives and friends gather in front of the house; inside, the shamans lay the novice on the ground and cover him with leaves and branches, placing the wing feathers of a chicken on his head. (This vegetable burial could be interpreted as a symbolic interment and the feathers as the magical sign of the mystical power to fly.[68]

Saint Oran's burial has a clear intention – to gain a more perfect knowledge of the spirit worlds (heaven and hell). By means of live burial, he gains experience of these otherworlds, and is able to report on their true nature upon his return to 'life'. A more clear metaphor for the shamanic journey would be difficult to find.

Live burial and isolation are sensory deprivation techniques at not too far remove from the primal Celtic *terbfeis*, in which the practitioner is wrapped in a bull's hide in order to restrict movement. Pennant records a more exact parallel of this early Irish prophetic ritual however:

> ...a family who pretended to oracular knowledge practiced these ceremonies. In this country is a vast cateract whose waters, falling from a high rock, jet so far as to form a dry hollow beneath, between them and the precipice. One of these impostors was sewed up in the hide of an ox, and, to add terror to the ceremony, was placed in this concavity; the trembling enquirer was brought to the place, where the shade, and the roaring waters, increased the dread of the occasion. The question is put, and the person in the hide delivers his answer. And so ends this species of divination known as *Taghairm*.[69]

Decoding Pennant's sceptical and emotive language, we are able to see both the pagan and shamanic significance of this ritual. Perhaps in these techniques we are witness to the continuation of a tradition ubiquitous in the shamanic world.

Gaelic Chant and Possession

The use of chant in a religious context is well attested in Gaelic tradition, and is still practiced in Presbyterian churches on Lewis to this day. Gaelic psalm singing has a quality unique to itself: the precentor leads the chant by singing the psalm line by line with the congregation singing it back to him as he goes. MacLeod describes the technique:

Melodic modifications do occur in some of the tunes in the process of adaptation to Gaelic modal patterns, but these are not to be taken as the only cause of the unaccustomed listener's confusion as he tries to link the printed tune with the Gaelic version. There is no clear break between the precentor's chant and the beginning or end of the original musical text; the singing is very slow, possibly to convey the solemnity of the occasion even if the psalm is a joyful one; and passing notes and grace notes are introduced to decorate the basic melody – but not to the extent of obscuring it, and the precentor's voice should keep the congregation together on the basic notes, which coincide with the beginnings of syllables.[70]

The effects of this kind of chant are described as an 'intensely moving experience'[71] – a testimony to its efficacy in invoking trance.

Of this style of singing, the Rev. Malcolm MacPhail remarked 'the singing at family worship was so general and continuous that it seemed unbroken from one end of the township to the other'.[72] The continuous nature of Gaelic psalm singing is important to highlight as it leaves little time to draw breath when sung along or in a small group. In such cases, shortage of breath can cause a light-headedness and, if continued for a significant period of time, can invoke the 'Eerie state' to which Lewis Carroll refers.

When listening to examples of Gaelic psalm singing, one cannot help but be reminded of the sound of Buddhists chanting mantras. By and large the Gaelic words of the psalm become indistinct, sacrificed to 'the ebb and the flow' of the tune itself. As a friend of mine from Lewis put it: 'you get lost in the tune, and eventually your body sways along with the murmuring of the psalms'. According to Kenneth Macleod, the later prayers and invocations in the *Carmina Gadelica* were 'recited in a curiously rhythmic monotone',[73] a description at not too far remove from depictions of Buddhist 'deep throat chanting'.

However, this is not the only type of trance invoking chant in evidence in Gaelic tradition. *Port-a-beul*, or 'mouth-music', is a song-style which uses repetition, a fast rhythm and a close rhyme scheme to create a sung chant. As opposed to the slow and graceful psalm chanting, *port-a-beul* are caillidh songs, often sung for entertainment and dancing. The fast pace of these chants again cause a shortage of breath. In Yogic meditation, manipulation of the breath (*prānāyāma*) is key to achieving a trance state.

>...this power enables the yogin to detach himself from the world and even in some measure to destroy it. Because yogic liberation is equivalent to completely breaking all ties with the cosmos; for a *jívan-mukta*, the universe no long exists ... it seems to us significant that Indian spirituality, seeking a means of metaphysical liberation, employed a technique of archaic magic reputedly able to abolish physical laws and play a part in the very constitution of the universe.[74]

Although this goes beyond the technique in evidence in both *port-a-beul* and Gaelic psalm singing, we can at least recognize a relative of this shamanic practice in effect.

An example of a *port-a-beul* from the *Carmina Gadelica* illustrates both the fast pace and repetition of vocabulary that typify this song style.

> *An Teòr tha os mo chionn,*
> *An Teòr tha os mo bhonn,*
> *An Teòr tha os mo bhos,*
> *An Teòr tha os mo thall;*
> *An Teòr a tha san talamh,*
> *An Teòr a tha san adhar,*
> *An Teòr a tha sna flathas,*
> *An Teòr a tha sa mhuir mhóir bhòrcaich.*[75]

> The Three who are over me,
> The Three who are under me,
> The Three who are over me here,

103

The Three who are over me yonder,
The Three who are in the earth,
The Three who are in the air,
The Three who are in the heavens,
The Three who are in the great pouring sea.[76]

This particular example of *port-a-beul* places it in a religious context – a supplication to 'the Three' for protection. At first glance, it may appear that 'the Three' points towards the Christian Trinity of Father, Son and Holy Spirit; however the Gaelic term for the Trinity is *an trianaid*, as used throughout Gaelic hymnody. Given the Gaelic proclivity for addressing things by their proper names, it is likely that '*an Teòr*' refers to something quite different.

The answer comes in the second half of the chant – 'the Three who are in the earth'; 'the Three who are in the air' and 'the Three who are in the great pouring sea': i.e. the three elements of earth, sea and sky – a well recognized spiritual theme from Old Irish literature. King Conchobar Mac Nessa, in an early version of the *Táin Bó Cúalnge* contained within the *Leabar na h'Uidre*, invokes these elements to hold him to account: '*Muir ara cendaib, in nem húasa mbennaib, talum foa cosaib* ... (I swear) By the sea before them, the sky above them, the earth beneath them'. A later version of the same tale found in the *Book of Leinster* has Súaltam, Cú Chulainn's father, recognise their power.

The function of this *port-a-beul* is to invoke the three elements for the purposes of encompassing. Called *caim* in the vernacular, encompassing has the effect of placing the protection of spiritual forces around an individual or group in order to keep them from harm. Its efficacy was seldom doubted, and was practiced by Catholics and Protestants alike. Many stories survive of how the *caim* charm protected an individual against malignant forces or persons. It was through the circulation of such tales that the superstition remained alive.

In making the 'caim' the suppliant stretches out the right hand with the forefinger extended while invoking the desired protection. The circle encloses the suppliant and accompanies him as he walks onward, safeguarded from all evil without or within.[77]

Perhaps most interesting in terms of our present study is the antiquity of this practice. In *caim*, we find perhaps the most perfect example of shamanic practice continued from pagan until Christian times. The modern day example of *caim* given above is contrasted against the Old Irish prayer *Faeth Fiada* (the 'Deer's Cry'), later incorporated into Saint Patrick's breastplate.

Críst limm, Críst reum, Críst im degaid,
Críst indium, Críst ísum, Críst uasum,
Críst desum, Críst tuathum,
Críst i llius, Críst i sius, Críst i n-erus,
Críst i cridiu cech duibi immumrorda,
Críst i ngin cech oín rodom-labrathar,
Críst i cech rusc nodom-dercathar,
Críst i cech cluais rodom-cloathar.[78]

Christ be with me, Christ before me, Christ behind me,
Christ within me, Christ beneath me, Christ above me,
Christ to the right of me, Christ to the left of me,
Christ in my lying down, Christ in my sitting, Christ
  where I stand
Christ in the heart of all who think of me
Christ in the mouth of all who speak to me,
Christ in the eye which beholds me,
Christ in every ear which hears me speak.[79]

Christian imagery aside, we can see the same function in effect. Despite a chronological separation of more than a thousand years, the similarities between the two prayers are striking. If, like modern scholars popularly believe, we accept that the *Faeth Fiada* is pre-Christian; then we must also recognise the primal elements found in its Gaelic descendant.

We also find *caim* in a druidic context, as depicted in the medieval Irish tale *Scéla Eogain*:

> When Cormac was born, the Druid-smith Olc Aiche put five protective circles about him, against wounding, against drowning, against fire, against enchantment, against wolves, that is to say against every evil.[80]

Of particular interest in a shamanic interpretation of *caim* are the second, fourth and seventh lines of the *Faeth Fiada*: more specifically *Críst indium* ('Christ within me'); *Críst i n-erus* ('Christ where I stand'); and *Críst i cech rusc nodom-dercathar* ('Christ in every eye which beholds me'). Given that the mode of practice for encompassing prayers was probably chant, these lines indicate the possibility of ritualised possession. Certainly in later Christian times this would not have been a wholly unpalatable notion, as this account from the *Book of Arran* illustrates:

> Almost at every meeting, when a clergyman or other person, who they judged to have the Spirit, presided, great numbers, especially of women and children, were moved in a most extraordinary manner, uttering strange cries, trembling and falling into larity. . . Multitudes flocked to the services, they travelled ten or fifteen miles to attend, they so crowded the building as to tread on each other; services were prolonged into private houses and barns, and some even spent whole nights in such ecstasy.[81]

In his tour of the Hebrides in the late eighteenth century, Dr. Johnson relates a story of a famous Skye seer who would faint, and upon recovery would recite prophetic visions he had received.[82] This description indicates possession.

Pennant also records an interesting account of highland 'second sight'. His narrative is from the point of view of the sceptic:

> These pretenders to second sight, like the Pythian priestess, during their inspiration fall into trances, foam at the mouth, grow pale and feign to abstain from food for a month, so over-powered are they by the visions imparted to them during their paroxysms.[83]

These descriptions replicate that of the *Awenyddion* given in the previous section.

Possession is a frequent experience in Vodou rituals. Whilst Eliade did not think Vodou could be classified as a shamanic phenomena in its strictest sense, he felt that the 'morphology of the trance, the techniques of possession, the initiatory rites etc., form invaluable documents for comparison with shamanistic phenomenon'.[84] In Vodou, much like the Arran services depicted above, the possessed are:

> ...protected from the possible effects of their frenzy by the crowd which surrounds them ... if they fall, arms are ready to catch them ... their modesty is shielded: a woman rolling on the ground, convulsed, is followed by other women who see to the disorders of her dress.[85]

It is thought that such sympathetic concern creates an atmosphere of trust and security 'conducive to total abandon in the state of trance'.[86]

In Vodou tradition, trance possession is seen in terms of equine symbolism. The *lwa*, or divinity, is seen as the rider; the possessed person as the mount. In the act of possession, or *tso* (literally meaning 'to snatch'[87]) results in the possessed's body contorting and bucking like a wild horse. A modern description of this phenomenon records:

...they pray, clap, and sing until the crowd is sufficiently 'heated up' to entice a Vodou spirit to join the party, to 'ride' Alourdes. In a trance state from which she will later emerge with little or no memory of what has transpired, her body becomes the 'horse' of the spirit, her voice the spirit's voice, her words and behaviour those of the spirit.[88]

Such descriptions offer up other possibilities for trance possession in Gaelic folklore and oral literature. From this point of view, any reference to riding or being ridden could be a metaphor for spirit possession.

We see a possible reference to this in a superstitious tale from Perthshire:

Campbell records how a young tailor, named Cumming, from Rannoch in Perthshire, fell into a wasting sickness. He told people that his terrible state was caused by witches who used to come to him at night and change him into a horse, on which they then proceeded to ride through the air to Edinburgh and back. In the morning he was completely exhausted. The belief that witches turned men into horses for their own purposes and rode them until they were almost dead is widespread, and has many variants.[89]

There are a number of other possible references to trance possession in the later folklore, such as the keening women. According to some views, these women were more commonly associated with the *bean chaointe* (or 'death messenger'), also known as *bean sí*.[90] O'Brien has said that '...anyone who has heard the keen will feel ... the keener is as one possessed. The tribe speaks through her, resenting, striving to undo the "vile subtraction", ultimately accepting it and falling back on propitiation to the departed.'[91]

There are also a number of tales which relate violence done to the living by spiritual entities. A story told to Martin Martin on Lewis depicts a man being beaten by a spirit so severely that the victim was bedridden for fourteen days afterwards. Of this incident, Ross surmises that 'beating by a supernatural being is an ancient Celtic belief'.[92] We see this motif prominently in *Serglige con Culainn*, as well as other Old Irish tales.

As an ecstatic phenomenon, possession is more clearly in evidence in early Celtic sacred practice; however a close inspection of later religious traditions and folklore reveal what one might regard as echoes of a more primal Celtic past.

Túathcháech and the Gaelic Sucking Doctor

The compound term *túathcháech* is often given to mean 'blind in the left eye' or 'having one evil eye'. The first part of the compound, *túath-*, has a wide range of meanings: it covers 'northern', (on the) left, 'perverse', 'evil' or 'wicked'. There are strong associations of the north with the supernatural – Ó Giolláin explains:

> In Irish *thiar* means 'west', but also 'back', 'behind', so that in directional terms having one's back to the west means having one's left hand side to the north (where the sun never shines) and one's right to the south.[93]

The negative associations with the north and left are explicitly shown in the latter meanings of *túath-*, 'wicked', 'evil' etc. To judge by its derivatives *túaithe* 'witchcraft', *túathach* 'witch' etc. this sinister quality also connects to the supernatural.

The second part of the compound, *cháech*, is often translated as 'one-eyed', 'purblind' or 'dimsighted'. According to Stokes, 'squinting' is another meaning of *cáech*.[94] Thus *túathcháech* is often given as 'blind in the left eye'.

Of literary occurrences of *túathcháech*, Toner concludes that 'the earliest recoverable form appears to be Old Irish (possibly eighth century) but this was evidently transcribed, with some modernization, in the Middle Irish period'.[95] In *Aided Con*

Culainn, despite having perceived evil omens, Cú Chulainn sets out to do battle. Before he leaves, he utters a prophetic speech in which he refers to his enemies:

> *Ammiti tuathchaecha taircebat mo milliud...*[96]
>
> *Túathcháech* witches will bring about my destruction...[97]

Later in this episode, whilst Cú Chulainn is on his way to visit his foster-mother, he encounters the *túathcháech* witches:

> *Co n-accai ní na teora ammiti túathchaecha ara chind forin tsligid.*[98]
>
> He saw something: the three *túathcháech* witches stood before him on the road.[99]

The witches are depicted as cooking dog-meat with poisons and spells on a fire. One witch offers the dog flesh to Cú Chulainn with her left hand, who places it under his left thigh. His hand and thigh then lose their usual strength. At the end of the narrative, the last mention of *túathcháech* occurs when Cú Chulainn's wife laments that the witches have destroyed her husband. It is *geis* for Cú Chulainn to eat the flesh of his totem, but it is also *geis* for anyone to refuse hospitality. Through this predicament, Cú Chulainn was undone.

Túathcháech is often associated with dismemberment. In one later version of *Aided Con Culainn*, queen Medb makes the six children of Calatín into *túathcháech* witches by removing 'their right legs and their left arms from them'.[100] This mutilation is not unique to this text alone. In *Acallam na Senórach* three red, poisonous men from the *Tuatha Dé Dánnan* go to Ireland to destroy the *fiana* in revenge for the murder of their father. The description of their acts involves mutilation – 'the removal of feet, hands, and eyes'.[101] The adjective *túathcháech* is found when they are banished. They are described as:

a tri náimhde tuathchaecha lesbaccach[a] leisbréna, lethtsúilecha leithcherra...[102]

the three *túathcháech*, lame-thighed, foul-thighed, one-eyed, half-maimed enemies...[103]

Such depictions marry *túathcháech* with the malevolent practice of *corrguinech*. Another compound word, *corrguinech* is invoked when casting the 'evil eye' in the tales. Without going into too much detail, *corr* is given to mean 'crane' or 'heron' – birds which are want to stand on one leg. Interestingly, Adomnán associates Saint Columba with cranes. The second element, *guin*, means 'wounding'; so the entire word may be translated as 'crane-wounding posture'. When a person adopts *corrguinech*, they stand on one leg, close one eye and stretch out one hand.[104] This could be in imitation of the crane, lending this practice a clearly shamanic air; however it is also reminiscent of depictions of the mythical Irish 'Fomorians', or one eyed, one-legged giants. Again this lends a sinister aspect to the practice.

In the western isles we can see the descendants of *túathcháech* and *corrguinech* in the casting of the evil eye. According to folklore, spiritual malice could be transferred to an individual by 'glancing'. With just one look, an individual may cast the *droch shùil* or 'evil eye'.

A young intelligent lady was lately in a house in the village of Golspie, the occupant of which, mourning over the dying of her fowls, said she suspected it was the result of the Evil Eye of Mrs.X., a neighbour. The next day, being in the same house, another neighbour came in carrying a growing plant, which she presented to the complainer, saying: 'Mrs. X. told me that you had your eye on this, and ever since it has done no good; the leaves have been withering and falling off. now! - there it is to you! keep it![105]

111

This method of cursing is seen to be directed by the eye – pointed in the direction of the recipient of the practitioner's malice. This is reminiscent of the aboriginal pointing bone or stick, thought to cause death to anybody it singles out.[106] The rite involves a sung incantation, and may sometimes involve the adoption of a particular stance or posture.

The shaman's ability to curse or even kill is put down to the assistance of the spirits. In 'singling out' an individual – either through the evil eye, or by the pointing bone – the shaman informs the spirits which person to attack. After this identifying gesture, the shaman need do nothing more, allowing the magic to work on its own.

o0o

Conversely, the shaman is also responsible for spiritual healing in their community, indeed magical healing appears to be the principle function of the shaman in Central and North Asia.[107] This is reflected by Beith in her observations on traditional healing in the Scottish highlands: 'Gaelic medicine is deeply interwoven into the story of the Gael as a whole.'[108] In traditional shamanic cultures, healing can take two forms: the restoration of power which has been lost and the removal of power intrusions. Harner appears to place greater emphasis on the latter form of healing,[109] so this is where we shall look for evidence of shamanic healing in Gaelic traditions.

Healing extraction involves the removal of harmful power intrusions usually by sucking them physically out of the patient. As a technique, it is widely used in Australia, Siberia and North and South America.[110] The intrusion may be seen as a spiritual poisoning, usually manifesting in the form of a malignant creature. Harner reports that 'if the patient has a harmful power intrusion, the shaman suddenly sees one of the following: voracious or dangerous insects, fanged serpents, or other reptiles and fish with visible fangs or teeth'.[111] With this in

112

mind, it is interesting to note that on Lewis, a large number of charms exist to counteract 'adder bite' even though there are no adders on the island. This leads one to suppose that this is not a physical poisoning.

Healing extraction is enacted in three stages. First, power must be established over the harmful intrusion so that the shaman may remove it. Secondly, the intrusion must be 'sucked out' or otherwise removed from the patient. Finally, it must be neutralised or safely disposed of.

We see this technique performed in the traditional healing practices of the western islands from a number of sources. Carmichael's *Carmina Gadelica* records a number of instances of healing extraction for a number of maladies. In each case, the three stages of establishing power, removing power, and neutralising power are observed. In the case below, power is established over a spiritual intrusion which has caused chest seizure.

Tha neart gil agam ort,
Tha neart gréin agam ort,
Tha neart dil agam ort,
Tha neart déir agam ort,
Tha neart lir agam ort,
Tha neart léir agam ort,
Tha neart rioll agam ort,
Tha neart reul agam ort,
Tha neart cruinn agam ort,
Tha neart speur agam ort,
Tha neart nùmh agam ort,
Tha neart nèamh agam ort,
Tha neart nèamh agus neart Dhé agam ort,
Tha neart nèamh agus neart Dhé agam ort.

Power of moon I have over it,
Power of sun I have over it,
Power of rain I have over it,
Power of dew I have over it,
Power of sea I have over it,

Power of land I have over it,
Power of stars I have over it,
Power planets I have over it,
Power of universe I have over it,
Power of skies I have over it,
Power of saints I have over it,
Power of heaven I have over it,
Power of heaven and God I have over it,
Power of heaven and God I have over it.[112]

As power is established over the intrusion by means of this chant, it is removed from the physical and spiritual bodies of the patient. Harner notes the use of song and chant in the establishment of power over harmful entities in the preliminaries to healing extraction.

> When the shaman senses the particular location, he calls the two spirit helpers, either silently or in song, as he shakes his rattle steadily over the patient. When he sees the helpers approaching in the darkness, with his eyes still closed he wills them into his mouth. There they will capture and absorb the power intrusion as he sucks it out of the patient.[113]

After this, the Gaelic healer removes the intrusion through a series of hand gestures or by sucking. When the parasite is removed, it may be safely disposed of, as in the conclusion to the charm for chest seizure:

> *Trian air na clacha glasa dhìot,*
> *Trian air na beanna casa dhìot,*
> *Trian air na h-easa brasa dhìot,*
> *Trian air na niala lasa dhìot,*
> *Trian air na miala mara dhìot,*
> *Trian air na biasta facha dhìot,*
> *Trian air na criara carra dhìot,*
> *Trian air na liana cana dhìot,*
> *Trian air a' mhuir mhóir bhòrchaich -*
> *Is i féin is fear ga gu giùlan*
> *A' mhuir mhóir bhòrchaich,*

'S i féin is fear ga gu giùlan.

A portion of it on the grey stones,
A portion of it on the steep mountains,
A portion of it on the swift cascades,
A portion of it on the gleaming clouds,
A portion of it on the ocean whales,
A portion of it on the meadow beasts,
A portion of it on the fenny swamps
A portion of it on the cotton-grass moors,
A portion on the great pouring sea -
She's the best one to carry it,
Oh the great pouring sea,
And she's the best one to carry it.[114]

As the intrusion is removed, it is neutralised by means of rending into pieces and scattering it amongst the elements. The last four lines are significant here, as in traditional shamanic cultures spirit intrusions are usually neutralised by placing them in water.[115] Trevarthen speculates that 'because fire and physical heat are associated with power, placing the intrusion in water is believed to disempower it, to cool it down'.[116]

The healing and curative powers of water are well attested in Gaelic folklore. One particular cure for the evil eye (which may also be seen as a spirit intrusion) was to sprinkle the patient with water, and then as the water became contaminated with the curse, it would be poured away either on the fire or on a rock by the front of the house.[117]

Ross relates another example of healing extraction from the island of Gigha, which was intended as a cure for swelling of the glands (*màm*):

> A magical incantation was apparently whispered over the blade of a knife or axe – steel was an essential ingredient in the cure – which was then held close to the mouth, and finally the blade was placed upon the swollen part. The swelling was then crossed and divided into nine or some other odd number; each time one of

these divisions of the swelling was crossed with the steel, the blade was pointed towards a hill ... In this way the swelling of sickness was transferred to the natural swelling of the hill and this performance was believed to be an infallible cure. When the swelling had been divided up and counted in this way, the blade was pointed towards the ground and the following words were said: 'The pain be in the ground and the affliction in the earth.'[118]

In another healing chant, we see that outside spiritual agencies are employed for the purposes of healing. After a short invocation to a named spirit, spiritual healing can occur in much the same way as the shamanic 'power song' is enacted.

A Léigh m'anama
Gleidh mi anmoch,
Gleidh mi moch,
Gleidh mi nòn,
An còrsa garbha,
Comhn is tearmaid
Mo shealbh a nochd.
  Tha mi sgìth is clì is cearbach,
  Dìon mi o chealg 's o lochd.[119]

You healer of my soul,
Keep me at evening,
Keep me at morning,
Keep me at noon,
On rough course faring,
Help and safeguard
My means this night.
  I am tired, astray, and stumbling,
  Shield me from deceit and harm.[120]

Many shamans report feeling ill or drained after healing extraction ceremonies, as they have taken on the sickness of the patient for a little while during the process of removal (in the case of the sucking doctor, they have sucked it into their mouth before spitting or vomiting it out into water). This is also a theme we see reflected in later Gaelic folklore. One healer, after using the 'charm of the thread' to cure the evil eye, often felt ill afterwards and had to take to her bed for days. She was also a midwife, and said that 'when called to attend' she felt herself 'helpless in the grasp' of a power or being which controlled her. She attributed her successes in this field to this power.[121]

o0o

Cursing and healing are only two manifestations of shamanic power in traditional cultures, although they are the most common. I do not have space to go into all the other aspects of shamanic consciousness in Celtic and Gaelic societies, and much more research and translation work is required in these fields before a satisfactory study can be made. Nevertheless I believe that the shamanic applications of *túathcháech*, *corrguinech*, the *droch shùil* and healing extraction, point toward a recurring pattern in Gaelic and older traditions; one which recognises the role of the shaman.

Binding the Threads

From these images of Gaelic shamanism, a more general trend and evolution emerges. In primal Celtic times we can see a structured use of shamanic power, clearly in evidence through the agency of the shaman proper. In these later times, we can begin to see the breaking down of this model – the shaman no longer occupies a prominent place within the community. Whilst I believe that shamanism is still clearly in evidence in Gaelic spiritual practice, the shaman probably was not.

In our search for the shaman in the Gàidhealtachd we have found the remnants of specific shamanic rituals and practices – some of which (like encompassing and *túathcháech*) have clearly survived since pagan times. Despite this, however, it is much harder to find examples of people who possess *samildánach* – the range of skills required of the shaman.

The reason for this is two-fold. Firstly, later spiritual movements have taken over the preserve of religious authority. In primal Celtic times we see that the druids are the specialists in the Sacred, and as such some are seen to employ ecstatic visionary means in their worship. However, as this role was subsumed by the Church, shamanic modes of practice were no longer sanctioned by the prevailing spiritual authorities.

This leads us to the second reason: as paganism and shamanism became increasingly persecuted and driven out, shamanic practice became more individual and diverse. To this end, later practitioners would often specialise in a particular shamanic trait: such as healing extraction (in the example of the Gaelic sucking doctor) or in the ascetic practices of the Celtic saints.

Whilst the role of the shaman may have begun to break down in later practices, the concept and practice of shamanism is still very much in evidence. A degree of cultural recognition is also illustrated in the widespread 'superstitious' belief in the efficacy of dream signs, curses, spiritual healing and the *dà shealladh*, or 'two sights'. An argument against this, however, is that many of the accounts of such practices are included as 'curiosities' or as old customs. Carmichael said of the tradition keepers and reciters with which he came into contact 'they are almost all dead now, leaving no successors'.[122]

In the end, however, we may still speak meaningfully of a shamanism prevalent within the cultures and traditions of the western isles of Scotland. Where these practices are in evidence, they are clearly of the shamanic mould, in continuation of primal Celtic themes. When all of the threads of Gaelic shamanism are bound together, we find a rope strong enough to tie to the past, to the pagan traditions of our primal ancestors.

CONCLUSION

'To the end of ends...'

Turn your face to the sunlight and the shadows fall behind you.
                                        Traditional Maori proverb.

And so, just as many traditional Gaelic songs conclude with the first verse, we arrive again at the point where we began. I hope that in the publication of this book, a new perspective on both Celtic and Gaelic material may be born; one which recognises many inter-cultural similarities and replications which point toward a more primal, shamanic source. It is recognised that much of the material presented in these pages may be interpreted in other ways; that academia has – for too long – found it comfortable to study the Celts and Gaels in isolation, without reference to any other field of research. Many scholars have found trying to write academically on the subject of Celtic shamanism rather like singing lullabies to the wind. However, I believe that a shamanic interpretation is the only one which pulls sharply into focus all the elements included herein, allowing a more comprehensive and fundamental understanding of the ancient mind.

Anthropologists aren't celticists and archaeologists aren't psychologists: these are truths which reveal why a shamanic perspective has, until recently, been considered taboo in the academic mainstream. Celticists have, like the classical authors before them, lacked the correct anthropological terminology with which to frame their interpretations of primal Celtic culture. It is only in recent years that some scholars have tentatively begun laying the foundations: Nagy, Aldhouse-Green and Trevarthen especially are owed a great deal of thanks from the academic community for paving the way in this line of research.

To this end, we are able to take the Celts back to the roots of the tree. The Indo-Europeans are the common ancestors of many peoples in Western and Middle to Eastern countries.

Buddhists, Hindus and Christians, then, all represent branches of the same world-tree; the *axis mundi* which the shaman uses to travel from this world to the world yonder: a thought which should perhaps be borne in mind considering the political climate of today.

In unmasking the primal Celtic shaman we have been able to identify the shamanistic qualities of the Gaelic oral tradition – the descendants of their more primal ancestors. Through their songs and chants, the Gaels displayed a complete spectrum of shamanic activity: from shapeshifting and sensory deprivation to healing extraction and totemism. In some cases, the continuity of practice spanning more than a thousand years is noteworthy.

The shaman is a specialist in the Sacred; one who fosters a personal and interactive relationship with the spirits. The druids did this, and so did the Gaels. Perhaps it is time that we start to call a spade a spade, and discard those pretensions which characterise outdated scholarship. Perhaps it is time that we recognised that no culture exists in a vacuum, and that only through comparative techniques are we able to gain a truer perspective of the Celtic peoples.

To get to this point has not been easy, and the path forward is unclear. Much more research needs to be done in these fields – there is far too much material to be included in this book. It is hoped that *Singing with Blackbirds* will help point the way for any future Celticists and anthropologists – as a spirit once told a Siberian Samoyed shaman 'Shamanizing, you will find your way, by yourself'.[1] I hope that this work has gone some way toward achieving this goal. Alongside the works of those scholars brave enough to tread this path before me, I lay this offering at the feet of my ancestors, and can only hope that they will consider it a sacrifice worthy of them.

DANCING WITH RAVENS

Man … cannot learn to forget, but hangs on to the past; however far or fast he runs, that chain runs with him.

F. W. Nietzsche

The raven once in snowy plumes was drest,
White as the whitest dove's unsullied breast,
Fair as the guardian of the Capitol,
Soft as the swan; a large and lovely fowl
His tongue, his prating tongue had changed him quite
To sooty blackness from the purest white.

Ovid, *Metamorphoses*

D ancing the spirits is an old custom among shamanic
cultures. Harner testifies to its antiquity, stating that it is
'widespread and obviously ancient',[1] and cites a number of
examples drawn from classically shamanic cultures.

> The dancer's spirit finds its dramatized expression in
> dance steps, tempo, movements, miens and gestures: in
> the sneaking pace, then flying leaps of the ferociously
> yelling 'warrior,' or in the swaying trot of the plump,
> sadly weeping 'bear mother'; in the rubber-like reptilian
> writhing of the 'double headed serpent' … in the 'lizard'
> who sheds tears over his devoured offspring or in the
> mighty 'whale' who grabs smaller fish.[2]

Animal dancing in the shamanic world has, as its objective, the
unification of totem and practitioner. Oftentimes a shamanic
dance may emulate the behaviour of a specific animal,
highlighting to onlookers and witnesses the attributes the
shaman has adopted.

The experience of dancing the spirit is transformative, it
reawakens the primal self. This primitive need to reunite with
the animal is demonstrated by a number of chants and songs
accompanying the spirit dance ritual. One example, from the
Osage Indian song series, illustrates this: *The Rising of the
Buffalo Bull Men.*

> I rise, I rise,
> I, whose tread makes the earth to rumble.
> I rise, I rise,
> I, in whose thighs there is strength.
> I rise, I rise,

125

I, who whips his back with his tail when in rage.
I rise, I rise,
I, in whose humped shoulder there is power.
I rise, I rise,
I, who shakes his mane when angered.
I rise, I rise,
I, whose horns are sharp and curved.[3]

In this example, the practitioner becomes 'possessed' by the spirit of the buffalo, and sings of his prowess and mighty attributes. *The Rising of the Buffalo Bull Men* is indicative of a wider shamanic practice, and is therefore illustrative of the ritual generally.

oOo

On a visit to North Uist in the process of gathering material for his *Carmina Gadelica*, Alexander Carmichael and his wife came across a strange scene. So affected were they by what they saw, Carmichael saw fit to record his experience in the appendices to volume two of his book. For clarity, I have quoted this section in its entirety.

> There were ten or twelve ravens in all, I forget which, on the smooth green grass adjoining the dry strand, and about a hundred yards below where we stood. On a small elevation hard by stood a large, noble-looking raven, probably the MacCrimmon of his race, and piped a 'port-a-bial,' mouth-tune, loud, fast, and furious. To this all the other ravens responded by running, and hopping, and jumping rapidly and regularly from certain given points in two opposite directions, 'They reeled, they crossed' but I cannot say they 'cleekit' like the witches in old Alloway kirk. But they certainly went through certain movements and evolutions, now singularly the 'Reel of Tulloch', and now absurdly like the 'Lancer's Quadrille' ... Ultimately this strange dance - as I think I am justified in calling it - ceased, having lasted, from the time we noticed the birds first, some eight or ten minutes.[4]

It is interesting that this observation is included in a volume meant to disclose the traditions, chants, songs and invocations of the Gaelic people. The notion that Carmichael may have reported a shamanic ritual in progress was first put forward in 2005.[5] The comparison to the witches' dance at Alloway kirk is interesting, as recent research has shown that the witches' sabbat probably involved shamanic techniques of ecstasy.[6]

In the above rendition, we can see clearly that one 'large, noble-looking raven' appears to be co-ordinating the ceremony - perhaps the shaman in ritual costuming resembling the raven? In order to come to a better understanding of this theory, one must first understand how the spiritual realm is depicted in shamanic cultures. An illustration of this is given below in this Shuar shamanic song. The italics in square brackets indicate which reality the shaman is referring to:

> I am like Tsuni, I am like Tsuni, [*spirit reality*]. When I drink natema, all my body becomes cold [*physical reality*] and I easily suck out the *tsensak* [*spirit reality*]. I am always above the clouds, and thus I have power [*spirit reality*]. There is a very large body of water [*physical reality*]. Thus, I am like a great body of water ... [*spirit reality*]. Now I am going to become dizzy, [*physical reality*] I will see [*spirit reality*] when I have become intoxicated [*physical reality*].[7]

From this example, it is clear to see how cumbersome it would be for the shaman to differentiate between spiritual and physical realities in speech; therefore both are depicted simultaneously. This concept is reflected in the Scots Gaelic superstition *dà shealladh* / the 'two sights', which, in contrast to its more common mistranslation 'second sight' implies no hierarchy within the two worlds.

In the first section, *Druids and Drums: The Instruments of Ecstasy*, we have already seen that the bird represents the shamanic totem *par excellence*. In adopting the shamanic costume, one becomes what one displays.[8] To this end, it

127

appears that the ravens in Carmichael's report may have been totemic spirits represented by shamans in ritual costuming.

The raven dance is not unique to Gaelic culture alone, however. In *Aithed Muirne re Dubh Ruis*, the similarities between the Kwakiutl Indians and primal Celtic culture are observed (see part one). In Carmichael's record, perhaps we are witness to a further intercultural parallel.

> The Kwakiutl Indians are a tribe confined to a slender strip of coastal water, sounds and inlets, and hundreds of densely forested islands and outcroppings of rock between the western coast of British Columbia and Vancouver Island in Canada. Roughly twenty indigenous tribal groupings occupy this territory between Campbell River and Smith Sound... A long recognised shamanic culture, the Kwakiutl are perhaps most famous for the *hamatsa* cannibal dancers, together with the elaborate ritual masks employed in their ceremonies.[9]

Most interestingly for this case study, however, is an account by Rohner and Rohner, published in 1970, of the 'raven dance' ceremony. This is part of a larger ritual which sees the performance of a number of animal dances including the mountain goat and the ermine.

> The first performance after supper was the Raven dance... The Raven appeared ... danced briefly and a second Raven appeared. They danced, one at each side of the fire. In certain poses (for example, when kneeling) one called to the other and the second answered, both vocally and with a clapping of the beak of the mask... The dance itself involved a continuous fast rhythm and a constant change of head and body movement. Their feet followed the rhythm but their hands and head did not perform the same movements.[10]

In this account, the costumed dancers are referred to not as practitioners in masks and costuming, but as 'Ravens'. It is clear that the dancers were not birds, however, as the ritual mask is referred to in the process of imitating bird calls.

We know from *The Language of Birds* in section three that imitation of bird calls was a widespread phenomenon in Gaelic oral literature. Just like Carmichael's account, the Kwakiutl raven dance is described as energetic, with a 'fast rhythm' which is kept by one individual (the 'large, noble-looking raven').

The Gaelic word for 'raven' is *fitheach,* a word which appears to encapsulate the words for 'omen' or 'augury' and 'bird'. It is fitting, then, given its association with spiritual traditions, that the raven would be chosen to represent the shamanic animal dance in the western islands. Green supports this theory, observing that the black plumage of the raven may have given rise to them being seen as 'messengers from the Otherworld'.[11] This would serve as a perfect metaphor for the shamanic ability to cross between spiritual and physical dimensions.

Dances in imitation of birds are not uncommon in later Gaelic traditions. Iain F. Campbell was witness to a dance called *cailleach an dùdain* ('dance of the smoky owl'); and dances such as *cath nan coileach* ('the battle of the cocks') and *ruidhleadh nan cuileach dubha* ('the reel of the black cocks') were traditionally performed on St. Michael's Night.[12] There is also a well known piping tune called 'The Desperate Battle of the Birds', which seeks to imitate the calls of many different bird species, and was initially meant as an accompaniment to *ceilidh* dancers.

Alexander Carmichael was born in Lismore, off the coast of Argyll, in 1832. As a Gael himself, he can be seen as an 'insider' in Gaelic tradition, and would therefore be fluent in any shamanic modes of reference and speech prevalent in these areas. As such, we would not expect Carmichael to refer to his ravens as 'men in costume and masks', as his frame of reference would come from the inside, as it were.

Given the previous research highlighted by this book, it would be foolish not to allow for a shamanic interpretation of Carmichael's record. In the end, the truth of Carmichael's experiences may never be known. However, given both Gaelic and intercultural precedents, it is just possible that he may have been witness to a shamanic spirit dance in honour of the raven totem. Unfortunately, without the benefit of a modern day shaman to undertake a journey into the memory of the past, the problem remains in the realms of speculation.

APOLOGIA

On Bananas and the Nature of Celtic Shamanism

E arly on in this study I encountered a lot of hostility from a number of groups which took exception to my research. Whilst these groups appeared to recognise that both primal Celtic and later Gaelic culture and spiritual practice did employ both visionary and ecstatic means; their objections arose from the terminology I chose to apply to such customs. This was founded on the basis that 'shamanism' as a linguistic term is neither a Celtic nor a Gaelic ethnonym. I rapidly became aware that such views were not the province of small, fanatical Gaelic purist groups, but represented something of a mainstream opinion in modern Celtic studies. I hope to address these concerns here, in order to put to bed such notions - allowing a holistic approach to the investigation of these concepts.

Arguments against the use of 'shaman' and 'shamanism' as ethnological terms appear to be founded on the notion that they are not derived from a Celtic language. If we were to restrict its use merely to it's native culture, then only Tungusic shamans could be defined as such. It is interesting to note that Tungusic has no concept of 'shamanism' - merely of the shaman or shamanka (female shaman) as embodied in the practitioner. Following this logic to its natural conclusion, we can no longer use the term shamanism in relation to any other culture: Buryat, Altaian, Kwakiutl and so on.

Restricting our vocabulary in this way makes an exercise in intercultural comparison both awkward and limited. Without an umbrella term, how are we able to hold one technique up against the other? In order to academically 'prove' the existence of Celtic shamanism we must find classically shamanic parallels - if a traditionally recognised shamanic culture is engaged in a certain activity which anthropology recognises as shamanic, and Celtic culture is found to also be engaged in such activities; then we have a basis for argument. I need a term to compare the practices of the Kwakiutl hamatsa and the Irish *gelta*. I need a term to compare the Buryat shaman's and Cú Chulainn's visionary experiences. I need a term to compare the spirit dance with rituals found to be taking place in latter day Coll and Uist. In short, I need 'shamanism'.

In arguing this point over email recently, I was told flatly that using this term in reference to either Celtic or Gaelic traditions was 'cultural rape'; that in Gaelic, there are a wealth of terms to describe the 'shamanic' elements inherent within its culture. I was told that 'we wish to be precise', and use the correct terminology. There are a number of issues here, not the least of which the issue of linguistic integrity. It is impossible to be a cultural and linguistic purist. Language is fluid and dynamic, it changes constantly.

I was once told by a Gaelic teacher that there are no loan-words in the Gaelic language, that everything was pure Gaelic. In response, I asked him what the Gaelic for banana is. He replied 'banana'. Are we to stop talking about bananas in Gaelic, even stop eating them, simply because they are not indigenous?

When vocabularies expand, languages borrow from each other. English has absorbed a great deal of 'foreign' words, and so has Gaelic. There are a number of terms in the vernacular which refer to specific ecstatic practices (such as *imbas forosnai*; *tenm laida* etc); but the fact remains that the native modern Gaelic word for the body of techniques anthropology calls 'shamanism' is 'shamanism'. It's a loan-word from English which finds its etymology in Tungusic.

In summary, then, I will continue to use this term in respect of Gaelic and Celtic cultures. In so doing I hope to take a holistic approach to our sources, encompassing the fields of archaeology, Celtic studies, anthropology, psychology etc. in order to better understand the mindset of a people chronologically removed from ourselves. In this way, we are able to make cultural comparisons with other shamanic tribes and peoples, enriching our understanding of our own ancestry.

NOTES

Introduction

1 For ease of reference, the masculine pronoun will be used in reference to the shamanic practitioner. In the native Tungusic, where the term originates, a female shaman is called a 'shamanka'.
2 Pokorny, 1908 – 9, p. 17 and Piggot, 1962, p. 118
3 Champion, 1995, p. 411
4 Cunliffe, 1997, p. 21
5 Sims-Williams, 1998a, p. 4
6 Sims-Williams, 1998b, p. 26
7 Sims-Williams, 1998b, p. 33
8 Walsh, 1990, p. 8
9 Eliade, 1964, p. 4
10 Rasmussen, 1929, pp. 118 – 119
11 Eliade, 1964, pp. 4 – 5
12 Hunter and Whitten, 1976, p. 12
13 Green, 1996c, p. 21
14 Eliade, 1964, p. 4
15 Caesar states that the immortality of the soul is chief amongst druidic teachings.
16 Kalweit, 1988, p. 235

Part One

1 Piggot, 1994, p. 100
2 Pliny (*Natural History*), 16.249
3 Commonly translated as the 'Romance of Mis and Dubh Ruis' I would argue that *Aithed* is more correctly translated as 'Flight'. This lends the tale a more shamanic air, possibly referring to the spirit flight each shaman must undertake to the spirit world. This hypothesis is strongly supported by the substance of the tale itself, which brings into play a great deal of avian symbology – for example Mis is said to be able to fly (see chapter three, *In Flight to the Spirits,* for further details on this point).
4 Ó Cuiv, 1952 – 1954, p. 333
5 www.celticshamanism.com/publications
6 Walens, 1981, p. 158
7 Cross and Slover, 1969, p. 179
8 Germania IX (Mattingly, 1970, p. 109) – italics mine.
9 Aldhouse-Green & Aldhouse-Green, 2005, p. 136
10 Eliade, 1964, p. 147
11 Trevarthen, 2003, p. 195
12 Eliade, 1964, p. 156
13 Eliade, 1964, p. 157

14 Shirokogorov, 1935, p. 152
15 Radlov, 1884, vol. II, p. 55
16 Eliade, 1964, p. 173
17 Ó Duinn, 1992, p. 5
18 Ó Duinn, 1992, p. 7
19 Ó Duinn, 1992, p. 9
20 Nagy, 1996, p. 6
21 Ó'Cuiv, 1952 – 4, p. 330
22 O'Donovan, 1868, p. 160
23 Eliade, 1964, p. 179
24 O'Donovan, 1868, p. 160
25 Low, 1996, p. 110
26 Beavitt, 1989, pp. 173 – 180
27 Wait, 1985, pp. 122 – 153
28 Cunliffe, 1986, pp. 155 – 171
29 Green, 1992, p. 126
30 Diodorus Siculus, V, 30, 2
31 Although the Gunestrup cauldron may represent the amalgamation of a number of cultures, we know that these warriors were Celtic by the presence of the Carnyx, or Celtic war horn. For more on this possibly shamanic instrument, see section two: *Gaining Possession of a Sacrality.*
32 Green, 1992, pp. 125 – 127
33 For chickens, see Eliade, 1964, pp. 350 – 351; for swans, see Eliade, 1964, pp. 39, 68, 155 and 176; for the goose in Altaic ecstatic ritual, see Eliade, 1964, pp. 191 – 195 and 203 – 204.
34 Ó Duinn, 1992, pp. 102 – 103
35 Wirz, 1922 – 1925, vol. II, p. 74
36 This closeness is the subject of the Case Study 'Dancing with Ravens' at the back of this book.
37 Footage from one of these ceremonies is held by St. Mungo's Museum of Religious Life in Glasgow.
38 Eliade, 1964, pp. 167 – 168
39 Eliade, 1964, p. 45
40 Armstrong, 1958, plate opposite p. 33
41 Trevarthen, 2003, p. 139
42 Stern, 1908, p. 189
43 Stern, 1908, p. 190
44 Powers, 1984, p. 56
45 Stern, 1908, p. 190
46 Green, 1992, pp. 121 – 122
47 Dillon, 1953a, p. 9

48 Piggot, 1962, p. 188
49 For more on this, see section three: *A Shaman in the Gàidhealtachd.*
50 Eliade, 1964, p. 462
51 Elaide, 1964, p. 160
52 Green, 1992, pp. 166 – 167
53 Harner, 1990, p. 60
54 Jilek, 1974, p. 92
55 Eliade, 1964, p. 289
56 Eliade, 1964, p. 289 – 290
57 Trevarthen, 2003, p. 135
58 Kopp, 2003, p. 126
59 *The Kilmartin Sessions*, 1997, cover leaflet, p. 9
60 Eliade, 1964, pp. 173 – 174
61 Eliade, 1964, p. 174
62 Diószegi, 1962, pp. 162 – 163
63 MacLennan, 2001, headwords *druma* and *dumach*
64 Royal Irish Academy, 1990, p. 500 headwords *rámach*, *rám* and *ráma*
65 Trevarthen, 2003, p. 211
66 Stokes, 1905, pp. 28 – 31
67 Trevarthen, 2003, p. 211
68 Aldhouse-Green & Aldhouse-Green, 2005, p. 109
69 Aldhouse-Green & Aldhouse-Green, 2005, p.128
70 Devlet, 2001, p. 47
71 Devlet, 2001, p. 47
72 *The Kilmartin Sessions,* 1997, cover leaflet, p. 1
73 *The Kilmartin Sessions,* 1997, cover leaflet, p. 6
74 Aldhouse-Green & Aldhouse-Green, 2005, p. 126
75 Trevarthen, 2003, p. 211
76 Green, 1997a, p. 18 – 'golden is in fact a mistranslation for *bronze*'
77 Eliade, 1964, p. 442
78 Hull, 1901, p. 439
79 Gantz, 1981, p. 193
80 Buckley, 1995, pp. 33 – 34
81 Cross and Slover, 1969, p. 198
82 Eliade, 1964, p. 128
83 Eliade, 1964, p. 177
84 Hull, 1901, pp. 434 – 444
85 Guest, 1906, pp. 263 – 264
86 Macalister, 1938 – 1956, pp. 110 – 113
87 my own translation, based on Macalister.
88 O'Dwyer, 2004, p. 20
89 Eliade, 1964, p. 180

90 Eliade, 1964, p. 180

Part Two
1   Eliade, 1964, pp. 85 – 86
2   Eliade, 1958a, p. 85
3   Rasmussen, 1929, pp. 118 – 119
4   Price-Williams and Hughes, 1994, p. 5
5   Métraux, 1942, p. 315
6   Loeb, 1929, p. 267
7   *De Situ Orbis* 3. 2.18
8   Carmichael, 1928, Vol. I, pp 2 – 3
9   *Vitae*, Introduction, p. 5
10 Eliade, 1964, p. 365
11 Eliade, 1964, pp. 365 – 6
12 Maclennan, 2001, headword *neul*
13 Ross, 2000, p. 119
14 Harner, 1990, p. 2
15 Wasson, 1968, p. 282
16 Rice, 1957, p. 90
17 quoted in Cunliffe, 1997, p. 190
18 Cooper and Johnson, 1984, p. 174
19 Cooper and Johnson, 1984, p. 174
20 Aldhouse-Green & Aldhouse-Green, 2005, p. 113
21 Buckley, 1995, pp. 28, 32
22 de Ruiter, 2003, p.27
23 reprinted in Spence, 1997, p. 95
24 Trevarthen, 2003, p. 113
25 Huun-Huur-Tu, 1993, from the insert to the CD
26 Buckley, 1995, p. 33
27 de Ruiter, 2003, p. 24
28 de Ruiter, 2003, p. 15
29 de Ruiter, 2003, p. 9
30 de Ruiter, 2003, p. 21
31 Eliade, 1964, p. 45
32 Stokes, 1894, pp.185 and following
33 Atkinson, 1901, p. 56
34 Chadwick, 1934-35, p. 103
35 Chadwick, 1934-35, pp. 110 – 111 & 118
36 Eliade, 1964, p. 371
37 Eliade, 1964, p. 104
38 Green, 1992, p. 25
39 Green, 1992, p. 52

40 Chadwick, 1934-35, p. 112, translated by Meyer
41 my own translation.
42 Cross and Slover, 1969, pp. 179 – 180
43 Campbell, 1987
44 Campbell, 1987, pp. 108 – 109
45 Chadwick, 1934 – 35, p. 126
46 Wasson, 1968
47 Chadwick, 1934 – 35,pp. 113 – 114
48 Chadwick, 1934 – 35, p. 119
49 Chadwick, 1934 – 35, p. 119
50 Meyer, 1912
51 Stokes, 1887, vol. I, p. 56
52 Chadwick, 1934 – 35, p. 133
53 Chadwick, 1934 – 35, p. 133
54 Tolstoy, 1985, p.140
55 Oesterreich, 1974, p. 254
56 Rasmussen, 1932, p.113
57 Tacitus, *Annals*, 14.30
58 MacRitchie, 1908 – 1909, p. 261, Ó Cathasaigh, 1977, also mentions
   cryptic variations of this account, pp. 70 – 72.
59 Trevarthen, 2003, p. 173 & pp. 219 – 284
60 Trevarthen, 2003, p. 276
61 Simbandumwe, 1992, p. 167
62 my own translation, heavily based on O'Rahilly, 1967, pp. 61 – 62;
   trans. pp. 201 – 202.
63 Oesterreich, 1974, p. 286
64 Eliade, 1958a, p. 98
65 Davis, 1995
66 Gray, 1983, pp. 32 – 33
67 Trevarthen, 2003, p. 176
68 Eliade, 1964, p. 4
69 Trevarthen, 2003, p. 64
70 Jaynes, 1976
71 Harner, 1990, p. 58
72 Matthews, 2002, p. 21
73 Fraser, 1887, p. 11
74 see Eliade, 1964, pp. 20 – 21 and Thompson, 1908, pp. 158ff
75 Eliade, 1964, p. 21
76 Eliade, 1964, p. 12 and p. 67
77 MacCulloch, 1911, p. 165
78 Green, 1993, p. 122
79 Green, 1993, p. 121

80 Silverman, 1967, p. 29
81 Silverman, 1967, p. 28 – 29
82 Royal Irish Academy, 1990, p. 181, headword *dán*
83 Royal Irish Academy, 1990, p. 181, headword *dán*
84 Trevarthen, 2003, pp. 158 – 161
85 Trevarthen, 2003, p. 159
86 Gray, 1982, pp. 38 – 39
87 Eliade, 1964, p. 19

Part Three

1 Carmichael, 1928, Vol. II, p. 298
2 see Green, 1996c, p. 21
3 Carmichael, 1940, Vol. III, pp. 270 – 271, translation by Carmichael
4 Carmichael, 1940, Vol. III, p. 271
5 Restall-Orr, 2002, p. 21
6 see Brunton, 1994, on www.shamanism.org/articles
7 Johnson, 1968, p.309; Ross also depicts this custom,
   see Ross 2000, p. 126
8 It is also significant that Hallowe'en, as Samhuinn, was thought to be
   the traditional New Year of the pagan calendar.
9 Eliade, 1964, p. 90
10 Harner, 1990, p. 60
11 Harner, 1990, p. 60
12 Elkin, 1945, pp. 74 – 75
13 MacKenzie, 1914, pp. 281 – 282
14 Carmichael, 1900 – 1901, Vol. I, pp. 52 – 53
15 MacKenzie, 1914, pp. 289 – 290.
16 MacKenzie, 1914, p. 290 – MacKenzie translates the Stewart's *riochd*
   as lions, but the Gaelic word for moth (*leòmann*) would appear more
   likely than *leòmhann* (lion).
17 Ross, 2000, p. 32
18 Ross, 2000, p. 27
19 Mackay, 1931, pp. 160 – 163, my own translations
20 Mackay, 1931, p. 163
21 Lonsdale, 1981, pp. 52 – 53
22 Erman, 1907, pp. 90 – 91
23 Eliade, 1964, p. 41
24 Eliade, 1964, p. 99
25 Carmichael, 1941, vol. IV, pp. 20 – 21
26 Carmichael, 1941, vol. IV, p. 6
27 Eliade, 1964, p. 99
28 Carmichael, 1941, vol. IV, p. 25

29 Diodorus Siculus, V, 31, 3
30 Métreaux, 1944, pp. 206 – 210
31 Loeb, 1929, p. 278
32 Lehtisalo, 1936 – 1937, pp. 23 ff
33 Eliade, 1964, p. 98
34 *The Kilmartin Sessions*, 1997, cover leaflet, p. 17
35 Blankenhorn, 1980, p. 31
36 *Spirit of the Outback*, 2000, from the cover leaflet & as illustrated in tracks one, six and eleven.
37 Carmichael, 1941, vol. IV, pp. 24 – 25
38 MacLennan, 2001, pg. 285 headword *seinn*
39 'with the ebb and with the flow' – the name given to a traditional form of Gaelic singing.
40 Carroll, 1893, p. 389
41 Often mistranslated as 'second sight', the Gaelic places no emphasis over one particular type of sight
42 Carroll, 1893, p. 389
43 MacKenzie, 1914, p. 72
44 Eliade, 1964, p. 128
45 Eliade, 1964, p. 129
46 Eliade, 1964, p. 84
47 Stirling, 1933, p. 140
48 Gougaud, 1927pp. 159 – 178
49 Ireland, 1997, pp. 52 – 53
50 Ireland, 1997, p. 53
51 Plummer, 1910
52 Herbert, 1988, p. 241
53 O'Kelleher, 1915, pp. 260 – 261
54 O'Grady, 1892, vol. II, p. 39
55 Stokes, 1905, pp. 10 – 11
56 Harva, 1938, p. 552
57 Harva, 1938, p. 493
58 Eliade, 1964, p. 412
59 Eliade, 1964, p. 412
60 Eliade, 1964, p. 437
61 Stokes and Strachan, 1903, p. 315
62 Carmichael, 1940, Vol. III, p. 49
63 Carmichael, 1928, Vol. II, p. 339
64 Carmichael, 1928, Vol. II, p. 339
65 my own translation.
66 Carmichael, 1928, Vol. II, p. 340
67 Eliade, 1964, p. 64

68 Eliade, 1964, p. 343
69 Pennant, quoted in Ross 2000, p. 59
70 MacLeod, 1994, p. 2
71 MacLeod, 1994, p. 2
72 *The Oban Times,* October 1898
73 Macleod, 1911-12, p. 127
74 Eliade, 1964, p. 413
75 Carmichael, 1940, Vol. III, p. 92
76 my own translation, based on Carmichael, 1940, vol. III, p. 93
77 Carmichael, 1940, vol. 3, p. 102
78 Carey, 1998, p. 134
79 my own translation, based on Carey, 1998, p. 134
80 Scott, 1990, p. 186
81 MacKenzie, 1914, p. 208
82 Ross, 2000, p. 44
83 Pennant, quoted in Ross, 2000, p. 58
84 Eliade, 1961 – 1962, p. 167
85 Métraux, 1972, p. 122
86 Métraux, 1972, p. 122
87 Lovell, 2002, p. 79
88 Brown, 2001, p. 5
89 Ross, 2000, p. 76
90 Lysaght, 1986, p.33
91 O'Brien, 1982, p. 248
92 Ross, 2000, p. 54
93 Ó Giollán, 1987, p. 72
94 Stokes, 1904, pp. 254 – 255
95 Toner, 1998, p. 87
96 Borsje, 2002, p. 10
97 my own translation
98 Borsje, 2002, p. 10
99 my own translation.
100 Ua Ceallaigh, 1935, p. 59
101 Borsje, 2002, p. 22
102 Borsje, 2002, p. 22
103 my own translation.
104 Cú Chulainn performs *corrguinech* in creating *geis*-binding oghams in
    Tain Bo Culaigne. Lugh also performs this art in *Cath Maige Tuired.*
105 MacLagan, 1902, pp. 8 – 9
106 see Cannon, 1942
107 Eliade, 1964, p. 215
108 Beith, 1995, pp. 2 – 3

109 see Harner, 1990, pp. 113 – 134

110 Harner, 1990, p. 116

111 Harner, 1990, p. 117

112 Carmichael, 1941, Vol. IV, pp. 256 – 257, with my own translation.

113 Harner, 1990, p. 121

114 Carmichael, 1941, Vol. IV, pp. 256 – 257 with my own translation.

115 Harner, 1990, pp. 121 – 122

116 Trevarthen, 2003, p. 178

117 Beith, 1995, p. 134

118 Ross, 2000, p. 108

119 Carmichael, 1940, Vol, III, p. 84

120 my own translation.

121 Mackinnon, 1908 – 1909, pp. 343 – 344

122 Carmichael, 1928, Vol. I, p. xxxvi

Conclusion

1 Popov, 1968, p. 143

Dancing With Ravens

1   Harner, 1990, p. 59

2   Jilek, 1974, p. 92

3   La Fleche, 1925, p. 209 – in the original series, each couplet is repeated once.

4   Carmichael, 1928, Vol. 2, p. 293

5   see Harris-Logan, 2005

6   see Ginzburg, 1992

7   Harner, quoted in Trevarthen, 2003, p.37, italics are Trevarthen's

8   Eliade, 1964, p. 179

9   Harris-Logan, 2005, pp. 16 – 17

10 Rohner and Rohner, 1970, pp. 100 – 102

11 Green, 1992, p. 126

12 Ross, 2000, p. 146

147

SELECT BIBLIOGRAPHY

Aldhouse-Green, M. & Aldhouse-Green, S.
2005   *The Quest for the Shaman: shape-shifters, sorcerers and spirit-healers of Ancient Europe*. London: Thames & Hudson

Armstrong, E. A.
1958   *The Folklore of Birds*. London: Collins

Atkinson, R.
1901   *Ancient Laws of Ireland*, Vol. 5. Dublin: Commissioners for publishing the ancient laws and Institutes of Ireland

Beavitt, P.
1989   'The Ethnoarchaeology of sacrifice: some comments on the visible and the invisible with respect to human contacts with the spirit world in Borneo.' in: Vigne, J. D. *L'Animal dans les pratiques religieuses: les manifestations materielles*, pp. 173-180. Paris: Anthropozoologica Troisième Numéro Special.

Beith, M.
1995   *Healing Threads: traditional medicines of the Highlands and Islands*. Edinburgh: Polygon.

Blankenhorn, V.
1980   *Calum & Annie Johnston: Songs, Stories and Piping from Barra*. Edinburgh: School of Scottish Studies.

Borsje, J.
2002   'The meaning of túathcháech in Early Irish texts.' in: *Cambrian Medieval Celtic Studies*, Vol. 43, Summer, pp. 1-24.

Boswell, J.
1968   *A Journey to the Western Islands of Scotland*. Menston: Scholar Press.

Brunton, B.
1994   *Tuva, land of evils: the foundations 1993 expedition to Tuva*. URL: http://www.shamanism.org/articles/1025228650.htm

Buckley, A.
1995   'And his voice swelled like a terrible thunderstorm: music as symbolic sound in Medieval Irish society.' in: *Irish Musical Studies*, Vol. 3, pp. 13-76.

Cameron, G.
1997   *Spiritual Crisis in Early Irish literature and later folk life*. URL: http://www.celticshamanism.com/thesis.html

Campbell, J.
1987   *The Power of Myth 3: The First Storytellers.* Television Programme.
        Alexandria: PBS.

Cannon, W. B.
1942   'Voodoo death.' in: *American Anthropologist,* Vol. 44 (new series),
        pp. 169-181.

Carey, J.
1998   *King of Mysteries: Early Irish Religious Writings.* Dublin:
        Four Courts Press.

Carmichael, A.
1900-1901 *Carmina Gadelica: Hymns and Incantations,* Vol. 1. Edinburgh:
        T&A Constable.
1928   *Carmina Gadelica: Hymns and Incantations,* Vol. 2. Edinburgh:
        Oliver and Boyd.
1940   *Carmina Gadelica: Hymns and Incantations,* Vol. 3. Edinburgh:
        Oliver and Boyd.
1941   *Carmina Gadelica: Hymns and Incantations,* Vol. 4. Edinburgh:
        Oliver and Boyd.

Carroll, L.
1893   *Sylvie and Bruno Concluded.* London: Macmillan & Co.

Chadwick, N. K.
1934-1935. Imbas Forosnai. *Scottish Gaelic Studies,*Vol. 4, pp. 97-135.

Champion, S.
1995   'Jewellery and Adornment.' in: Green, M., 1995, *The Celtic World,*
        pp. 411-419.

Clough, R. & Clough, D.
1997   *The Kilmartin Sessions: the sounds of Ancient Scotland* (CD cover
        leaflet). Kilmartin: Kilmartin House Trust.

Cooper, & Johnson,
1984   *Poisonous plants in Britain and their effects on animal and man.*
        London: Her Majesty's Stationary Office.

Cowan, J. G.
1992   *The Aborigine Tradition.* Shaftesbury: Element.

Cross, T. P. & Slover, C. H.
1969. *Ancient Irish Tales.* Dublin: Allen Figgis.

Cunliffe, B.
1997   *The Ancient Celts.* Oxford: Penguin.
1986   *Danebury: Anatomy of an Iron Age Hillfort.* London: Batsford.

Davis, W.
1995   'Shamans as Botanical Researchers.' in: Narby, J. & Huxley, F.,
       1995, *Shamans through time: 500 years on the path to knowledge.*
       pp. 286-290. London: Thames & Hudson.

De Ruiter, D.
2003   *Harmonic Overtones: magical vibrations in voice and music.*
       Havelte: Binkey Kok.

Devlet, E.
2001   'Rock Art and the material culture of Siberian and Central Asian
       Shamanism.' in: Price, N. S. *The Archaeology of Shamanism.*
       London: Routledge.

Dillon, M.
1953   *Serglige Con Culainn.* Dublin: Dublin Institute for Advanced Studies.

Diószegi, V.
1962   'Dream Learning and Individual Ritual Differences in Mohave
       Shamanism.' in: *American Anthropologist,* Vol. 59, Part 6,
       pp. 1036-1045.

Eliade, M.
1958   *Rites and Symbols of Initiation.* New York: Harper and Row.
1961-1962. 'Recent works on shamanism: a review article.' in: *History of
       religions,* Vol. 1, pp. 152-186.
1964   *Shamanism: Archaic Techniques of Ecstasy.* Princeton: Bollingen.

Elkin, A. P.
1945   *Aboriginal men of high degree.* Sydney: Australasian Publishing.

Erman, A.
1907   *A Handbook of Egyptian Religion.* London: Archibald
       Constable & Co.

Fraser, J. G.
       1886. *Totemism.* Edinburgh: Adam & Charles Black.

Gantz, J.
1981   *Early Irish Myths and Sagas.* London: Penguin.

Gougaud, D. L.
1927   *Devotional and ascetic practices in the Middle-Ages.* London:
       Burns, Oates and Washbourne.

Gray, E. A.
1982   *Cath Maige Tuired: the second battle of Mag Tuired*. Dublin:
Irish Texts Society.

Green, M.
1992   *Dictionary of Celtic Myth and Legend*. London: Thames & Hudson.
1993   *The Gods of the Celts*. Gloucestershire: Sutton.
1996   *Celtic Goddesses, Warriors, Virgins and Mothers*. London:
British Museum Press.
1997   *Exploring the world of the Druids*. London: Thames & Hudson.

Guest, Lady C.
1906   *The Mabinogion*. London: J. M. Dent & Co.

Harner, M. J.
1968   'The Sound of Rushing Water.' in: *Natural History*. Vol. 77, Part 6,
pp. 28-33.
1990   *The Way of the Shaman*. Tenth Anniversary Edition. San Francisco:
HarperCollins.

Harris-Logan, S
2005   *Dancing with Ravens: An Introduction to Gàidhlig Shamanism*.
Cambridge: Forewords Press.

Harva, U.
1938   *Die religiösen Vorstellungen der altaischen Völker*. Helsinki:
Folklore Fellows Communications.

Herbert, M.
1988   *Iona, Kells, and Derry*. Oxford: Clarendon Press.

Hull, E.
1901   'The Silver Bough in Irish Legend.' in: *Folklore*, Vol. 12,
pp. 431-445.

Huun-Huur-Tu.
1993   *60 horses in my herd, old songs and tunes of Tuva*. CD.
New York: Shanachie.

Ireland, C.
1997   'Penance and Prayer in Water: An Irish Practice in Northumbrian
Hagiography.' in: *Cambrian Medieval Celtic Studies*, Vol. 34,
Winter, pp. 51-66.

Jaynes, J.
1976   *The origin of consciousness in the breakdown of the bicameral mind*.
Harmondsworth: Penguin.

Jilek, W.
1974   *Salish Indian Mental Health and Cultural Change: psychohygienic and therapeutic aspects of the guardian spirit ceremonial.* Toronto: Holt, Reinhart and Winston of Canada.

Kalweit, H.
1988   *Dreamtime and Inner Space: the World of the Shaman.* Boston: Shambhala.

Lehtisalo, T.
1936-1937   'Beobactungen über die Jodler.' in: *Journal de la Société Finno-Ougrienne,* Vol. 48, Part 2, pp. 1-34.

Leob, E. M.
1929   'Shaman and Seer.' in: *American Anthropologist,* Vol. 31, Part 1, pp. 60-84.

Lonsdale, S.
1981   *Animals and the origin of the dance.* London: Thames & Hudson.

Lovell, N.
2002   *Cord of Blood: possession and the making of voodoo.* London: Pluto Press.

Low, M.
1996   *Celtic Christianity and Nature: early Irish and Hebridean tradition.* Edinburgh: Edinburgh University Press.

Lusk, J.
2000   'What does Aboriginal music sound like?' on: *Spirit of the Outback.* (CD Cover Leaflet). New Zealand: Manteca.

Lysaght, P.
1986   *The Banshee: The Irish Supernatural Death Messenger.* Dublin: Glendale Press.

Macalister, R. A. S.
1938-1956   *Lebor Gabála Érenn.* Dublin: Dublin Institute for Advanced Studies.

MacCulloch, J. A.
1911   *The Religion of the Ancient Celts.* Edinburgh: T&T Clark.

Mackay, J. G.
1931   'Cànain nan Eun.' in: *Scottish Gaelic Studies,* Vol. 3, pp. 160-187.

MacKenzie, W. M.
1914   *Book of Arran Vol. 2: History and Folklore.* Glasgow: Hugh Hopkins.

Mackinnon, D.
1908-1909 'A modern instance of Evil Eye.' in: *The Celtic Review*,
Vol. 5, pp.343-344.

MacLagan, R. C.
1992 *Evil Eye in the Western Highlands*. London: David Nutt.

MacLennan, M.
2001 *A pronouncing and etymological dictionary of the Gaelic language:
Gaelic-English, English-Gaelic*. Edinburgh: Mercat Press.

Macleod, K.
1911-1912 'Our Interpreter.' in: *Celtic Review*, Vol. 8, pp. 116-129.

MacLeod, M.
1994 *Gaelic psalms from Lewis*. Edinburgh: School of Scottish Studies.

MacPhail, M.
1898 Religion in the Isle of Lewis. *The Oban Times*.

MacRitchie, D.
1908-1909 'A new solution to the fairy problem.' in: *The Celtic Review*,
Vol. 6. pp. 160-176.

Matthews, J.
2002 *Celtic Totem Animals: make a shamanic journey and meet your
animal helpers*. Glastonbury: Gothic Image Publications.

McCarthy-Brown, K.
2001 *Mama Lola: A Vodou Priestess in Brooklyn (updated and expanded
edition)*. London: University of California Press.

Métraux, A.
1942 'Le Shamanisme araucan.' in: *Revista del Instituto de Antropología
de la Universidad nacional de Tucumán*, Vol. 2, Part 10,
pp. 309-362.
1944 'Le Shamanisme chez les Indiens de l'Amerique du Sud tropicale.'
in: *Acta Americana*, Vol. 2, Parts 3-4, pp. 197-219.
1972 *Voodoo in Haiti*. New York: Schocken Books.

Meyer, K.
1912 Sanas Cormaic. In: *Anecdota from Irish Manuscripts*, Vol. IV.
Max Niemeyer: Halle.

Nietzsche, F. W.
1869 *Nachlass* (Unpublished Notes).

Nagy, J. F.

1996 *A new introduction to Buile Suibhne: the frenzy of Suibhne: being the adventures of Suibhne Geilt; a Middle-Irish Romance*. London: Irish Texts Society.

O'Brien, M. C.

1982 The role of the poet in Gaelic Society. In: O'Driscoll, R., *The Celtic Consciousness*. Edinburgh: Cannongate. pp. 243-253.

Ó Cathasaigh, T.

1977 *The Heroic Biography of Cormac Mac Airt*. Dublin: Dublin Institute for Advanced Studies.

Ó Cuiv, B.

1952 The Romance of Mis and Dubh Ruis. *Celtica*, Vol. 2, pp. 325-333.

Ó Duinn, S.

1992 *Forbhais Droma Dámhgháire*. Dublin: Mercier Press.

O'Donovan, J.

1868 *Cormac's Glossary*. Calcutta: O. T. Cutter for the Irish Archaeological and Celtic Society.

O'Dwyer, S.

2004 *Prehistoric Music of Ireland*. Stroud: Tempus Publishing.

Ó Giollán, D.

1987 'Myth and History: exotic foreigners in folk belief.' in: *Temenos: Studies in Comparative Religion*, Vol. 23, pp. 59-80.

O'Grady, S. H.

1892 *Silva Gadelica*. London: Williams and Norgate.

O'Kelleher, A.

1915 'Betha Coluimb Chille.' in: *Zeitschrift für celtische Philologie*, Vol. 10, pp. 228-265.

O'Rahilly, C.

1967 *Táin Bó Cúailnge from the Book of Leinster*. Dublin: Dublin Institute for Advanced Studies.

Oesterreich, T. K.

1974 *Possession and Exorcism among primitive races, in antiquity, the Middle Ages, and Modern Times*. New York: Causeway.

Pennant, T.

1772 *A Tour in Scotland*, Vol. 2. Warrington.

Piggot, S.
1962 'Heads and Hoofs.' in: *Antiquity*, Vol. 36, pp. 110-118.
1994 *The Druids*. London: Thames and Hudson.

Plummer, C.
1910 *Vitae Sanctorum Hiberniae*. Oxford: E Typographeo Clarendoniano.

Pokorny, J.
1908 'The Origin of Druidism.' in: *The Celtic Review*, Vol. 5, pp. 1-20.

Popov, A. A.
1968 'How Serptie Djaruoskin of the Nganasans (Tavgi Samoyeds) became a shaman.' in: Diószegi, V., *Popular Beliefs and Folklore tradition in Siberia*, Bloomington: Indiana University Publications, pp.137-145.

Powers, W. K.
1984 *Yuwipi: Vision and Experience in Oglala Ritual*. Lincoln: University of Nebraska Press.

Price-Williams, D. & Hughes, D.
1994 Shamanism and altered states of consciousness. *Anthropology of consciousness*, Vol. 5, Part 2, pp. 1-15.

Radlov, W.
1884 *Aus Siberien: lose Blätter aus dem Tagebuche eines reisenden Linguisten*. Leipzig.

Rasmussen, K.
1929 *Intellectual Culture of the Iglulik Eskimos*. Report of the Fifth Thule Expedition 1921-24, Vol. 7, No. 1. Copenhagen: Gyldendalske Boghandel, Nordisk Forlag.
1932 *Intellectual Culture of the Copper Eskimos*. Report of the Fifth Thule Expedition 1921-24, Vol. 9. Copenhagen: Gyldendalske Boghandel, Nordisk Forlag.

Restall-Orr, E.
2002 *Living Druidry: magical spirituality for the wild soul*. Llandeilo: Cygnus Books.

Rice, T. T.
1957. *The Scythians*. London: Thames and Hudson.

Ross, A.
2000 *Folklore of the Scottish Highlands*. Stroud: Tempus Books.

Royal Irish Academy.
1990   *Dictionary of the Irish Language*. Dublin: Royal Irish Academy.

Scott, B. G.
1990   *Early Irish Ironworking*. Belfast: Ulster Museum Press.

Shirokogorov, S. M.
1935   *Psychomental Complex of the Tungus*. London: Kegan Paul & Co.

Silverman, J.
1967   'Shamans and acute schizophrenia.' in; *American Anthropologist*,
        Vol. 69, Part 1, pp. 23-31.

Simbandumwe, S. S.
1992   'Understanding the role of a prophet in Kimbanguist Hymns.' in:
        History of Religions, Vol. 32, pp. 165-183.

Sims-Williams, P.
1998a   'Genetics, linguistics and prehistory: thinking big and thinking
        straight.' in: *Antiquity*, Vol. 72, pp. 505-527.
1998b   'Celtomania and Celtoscepticism.' in: *Cambrian Medieval Celtic
        Studies*, Vol. 36, pp. 1-35.

Stern, L. C.
1908   'Ceangal nan tri Caol.' in: *Zeitschrift für celtische Philologie*.
        Vol. 6, pp. 188-190.

Spence, L.
1997   *Magical traditions of the British Isles*. New York: Llewelyn.

Sterling, M. W.
1933   Jívaro Shamanism. Proceedings of the American Philosophical
        Society, Vol. 72.

Stokes, W.
1887   *Tripartite Life*. Rolls Series: London.
1894   'On the Bodleian fragment of Cormac's Glossary.' in: *Transactions
        of the philological society*.
1904   'Hibernica XXVI: Etymologies., in: *Zeitschrift für vergleichende
        Sprachforschung auf dem Gebiete der indogermanischen Sprachen*,
        Vol. 37, pp. 253-261.
1905a   'Immacallam in dá Thuarad or Colloquy of the Two Sages.' in:
        Revue Celtique. Vol. 26, pp. 4-64.
1905b   *Félire Óengusso Céli Dé : The Martyrology of Oengus the Culdee*.
        London: Harrison and Sons.

Stokes, W. & Strachan, J.
1903 *Thesaurus Palaeohibernicus*, Vol. 2. Cambridge: Cambridge University Press.

Thompson, B.
1908 *The Figians*. London: William Heinman.

Tolstoy, N.
1985 *The Quest for Merlin*. London: Hamish Hammilton.

Toner, G.
1998 'The transmission of Tochmarc Emire.' in: *Eriu*, Vol. 49, pp. 71-88.

Trevarthen, G. A.
2003 *Brightness of Brightness: Seeing Celtic Shamanism.* Edinburgh: University of Edinburgh.

Ua Ceallaigh, S.
1935 *Rudhraigheacht*. Dublin: M.H. Macanghoil & a Mhac.

Wait, G. A.
1985 *Ritual and Religion in Iron Age Britain*. Oxford: British Archaeological Reports (British Series) No. 149.

Walens, S.
1981 *Feasting with Cannibals: an essay on Kwakiutl Cosmology.* New Jersey: Princeton University Press.

Walsh, R. N.
1990 *The Spirit of Shamanism*. London: HarperCollins.

Wasson, G. R.
1968 *Soma: Divine Mushroom of Immortality*. Danbury: Harcourt Brace Jovanovich.

Wirz, P.
1922-1925 *Die Marind-anim von Hollandisch-Süd-Neu-Guinea.* Hamburg: University of Hamburg Press.

INDEX

Adomnan 53, 111
Aes Dána 73-4
Aes Side xi, 73
Aillil 23, 31
Airmid 66
Alasdair 87-90
Altaians 11, 18, 73, 133
amanita muscaria 59
Amergin 36, 60, 73
ancestors xvii, 55, 61, 70-71, 118, 122
Andaman shaman 43, 88
animals (symbolism) 9, 11, 24, 25, 29, 34, 36-7, 57-8
animal totems *see* Totem (animal)
animism xiv, 4, 7, 8, 37, 68, 71, 79-81
Arran, Isle of 107
Atrebates xii
Awen 60
Awenyddion 60, 61, 62
ayahuasca 49
Badh Catha 16
bagpipe 53, 93
Balkåkra 31
berserkir 63
bicameralism 67
blood 4, 15, 80, 89
Brendan, Saint 87
Brigit 79, 80
binding *see* sensory deprivation
birds 11, 15-21, 26, 27, 87, 88, 92-4, 128
    imitation 90-94
    language 88, 90, 91
    Desperate Battle of the Birds 129
    Isle of the Birds 87, 89
bodhrán 38
Boyne, river 59
Breton (language) xii
caim 104-6
Caithness 57
Camonica Valley 57
cannabis 49

cannibalism 4, 15
Carmichael, Alexander 46, 79, 81, 90, 92, 99, 113, 126-30
carnyx 53, 57
Celts xii-xiii, 7, 16, 24, 33, 47, 49, 53, 54, 70, 71, 74, 121
Cernunnos 24
Cerridwen 36
chant 20, 27, 51-4, 60, 61, 93, 94, 96, 97-8, 102, 104, 106, 114,
   116, 125
chewing 57-8, 61
Ciumesti (Romania) 17
clúmh 4
Coll, Isle of 83, 134
Columba, Saint 53, 97, 99-100, 111
Colum Cille see Columba, Saint
Conchobar 34, 104
Cormac Mac Airt 13, 18, 20, 34, 63
Cornish (language) xii
corrguinech 111, 117
Costume (shamanic) 9-11, 15, 19-21, 25-6, 27, 35, 36-7, 38,
   82-5
Crane bag 33
Cú Chulainn 6, 34, 47, 48, 57-8, 63-5, 69, 104, 110, 134
dà shealladh 94, 107, 118, 127
dán 72-4
dance (animal imitations) 20, 25-6, 125-6, 129
Danebury 16, 57
death (symbolic / ritual) xv, 16, 43, 45, 47-9, 50, 55, 58, 59, 71,
   88-9, 95-6, 100-101
death-signs 86, 108
Delphi 46
Dian Cécht 66
dichetal do chennaib 55-6, 60, 61
didgeridoo 53, 93
Donn mac Midir 25
dordfhiansa 51-52
druid 3, 13, 18, 19, 23, 33, 37, 45, 46, 50, 52, 63, 66, 68, 128
Druid Rock 33
drum / drumming 12, 27-34, 35, 37-8, 49, 51, 94
éanchealtair 19-20
Egyptian 88

Eliade, Mircea xiv, xv, 38-9
entheogens *see* psychotropic drugs
evil eye 111, 115, 117
exstasis xiv, 55
Fianna 51, 110
filidh 14, 34, 56, 60, 61
Fionn MacCumhaill 18, 25, 33, 51, 58, 59, 69
fire 18-9, 26
flight (shamanic) 11, 18-20, 27, 36
Fomorians 111
Gaelic *see* Scots Gaelic
Gaelic psalm singing 101-2, 103
Gaels 46, 48, 92, 112, 121-2
gainisg 79
Gaul 7, 8
geis 57, 110
geltacht 4, 6, 14-5, 47, 134
Gigha, Isle of 115
Giraldus Cambrensis 18, 60
Goibhnhiu 8
Greek 7, 54, 74
Gundestrup cauldron 4, 5, 17, 24, 25, 28-9, 37, 57
Gussage All Saints 57
Hallowe'en 83
Halstatt xii
harmonic overtones *see* overtone harmonics
healing extraction 112-15, 117, 118
Hebrides 83, 106
imbas forosnai 48, 55-9, 61, 62, 98, 134
immersion 96-9
instruments (shamanic) 9, 10, 12, 13, 27, 29, 31-3, 34, 35, 38, 53
Iona, Isle of 33, 100
Irish (language) xii
Irish, Old (language) 3, 8, 20-21, 35, 36, 47, 48, 59, 60, 72, 80, 104, 105, 109
Isle of the Birds *see under* birds
keening 108
La Tène xii
Lewis, Isle of 97, 102, 108, 113

165

Lindow man 50
Lugh 73
lwa 46, 107
MacRoth 23, 31
Máelduin 87
Mannanan Mac Lir 18, 34
Manx (language) xii
masks 11, 19, 20, 21
Medh 23, 31, 110
Miach 66
Michael, Saint 129
Mis 4, 6, 14-15, 43, 67, 88, 90
mistletoe 33-4, 49-50
Mogh Roith 13, 17, 18-21, 26, 30-31, 62, 65, 68
Mona 62
Morgannwg, Iolo 52, 74
Mórrighan 16
mouth harp 53
music 27, 34-5, 38, 60
North Uist 126, 134
Nuadu 66
oak 34
Oisin 25, 69
Oran, Saint 99-100
orans posture 5
Orkney 57
otherworld xv, 38, 62, 65, 93, 94, 100, 129
overtone harmonics 51-4, 93
P-Celtic xii, xiii
Parisii xiii
Patrick, Saint 60, 97
pilililiu 92-4
port-a-beul 103-4
possession 14, 21, 46, 60-61, 64-5, 96, 106-8, 126
psychotropic drugs 49-51, 54, 59, 61, 94
Pythia 46
Q-Celtic xii, xiii
raven 16, 17-18, 20, 88, 126-9
riastraid 63-4
'ringing rocks' 32-3

riochd 85-7, 118
Roman 7, 24, 33, 45, 57, 62
Sabha 25, 69
Saints (Celtic) 23, 53, 79, 94, 95-6, 97-9
Santeria 82
School of Scottish Studies 90
Scots Gaelic (language) xii, 16, 21, 31, 39, 46, 47, 48, 57, 65,
    74, 79-81, 85, 87, 91, 92, 94, 99, 101, 104, 106, 122, 133-4
séance 12, 46, 91
seinn 93
sensory deprivation 21-3, 94, 95, 99
Shaman
    Araucanian 45
    Australian 21, 65, 69, 112
    Bori 61
    Buryat 73, 98, 133-4
    Bushman 58
    Carib 35, 95
    Chukchee 98
    Coast Salish 26
    Dyak 18
    Fijian 70
    Goldi 11
    Hamatsa 4, 5, 20, 85, 134; *see also* Kwakiutl
    Huchnom 45
    Iban (Borneo) 16
    Iglulik / Inuit xiv, 21, 27, 44, 61
    Indo-Tibetan shaman 99
    Jívaro / Shuar 49, 67, 95
    Korean 25
    Kwakiutl 4, 5, 20, 85, 128, 129, 133-4
    Lakota 22
    Lapp 18, 98
    Lolo shaman 34
    Marind 19
    Menangkabau 43
    Menomini 92
    Mentaweian 43
    Miwok 45
    Mongolian shaman 29, 37, 53

Naidu 56
Nicobar 100
Osage 125
Polynesian 56, 64-5
Pomo 45, 92
Samoyed 18, 88, 122
Siberian 18, 23, 30, 32, 35, 49, 70, 112, 122
Tungus 11, 25, 98
Turkish 25
Tuvan 30, 51, 53-4, 83
Ungarian 49
Yakut 84
Yogic 44, 103
Yuki 45
Zuni 26
Shetland 57
singing bowl 53
Skye, Isle of 106
soma 59
South Uist 93, 134
spirit world *see* otherworld
súan 35
Suibhne 14, 90
Taliesin 36
tarbfeis 22-3, 101
tenm laida 55-6, 59, 61, 134
throat singing *see* overtone harmonics
Tiree, Isle of 33
totem (animal) xv, 16, 26, 85-6
totem (plant) 34, 49-50, 86
totemism 67-71
trance xiv, 10, 12, 20-21, 24, 25, 30, 35, 43-5, 48-9, 51, 54, 56, 58, 59, 60, 61, 62, 63, 94, 98, 102, 107-8
túathcháech 109-10, 117
tuigen 15
Tungusic (language) xiv, 134
Vodou xvii, 46, 64, 82, 107
Welsh xii, 8, 52, 60
Winklebury 16

Lightning Source UK Ltd.
Milton Keynes UK
UKOW050254010612

193741UK00001B/1/A